STUDENT DISCIPLINE AND CLASSROOM MANAGEMENT

ABOUT THE AUTHOR

Jack Campbell is the author of *Individualizing Instruction for the Educationally Handicapped: Teaching Strategies in Remedial and Special Education*, published by Charles C Thomas. He has published articles in such journals as *Education, Planning for Higher Education, Educational Record, Mental Retardation, Education and Training of the Mentally Retarded,* and the *Journal for Special Educators of the Mentally Retarded.*

Since 1995 Jack Campbell has been the Class of 1964 Professor in the Education Department at Mount Saint Mary's College in Emmitsburg, MD. He has served as a visiting professor at St. Andrew's College in Scotland where he lectured, mentored, and conducted research. During the 17 years prior to 1995 he served as Provost and Vice President at Mount Saint Mary's College. From 1971 to 1978 he served as a professor in the special education program at the University of Nevada.

Currently he teaches undergraduate and graduate courses at Mount Saint Mary's in the areas of special education, educational psychology, assessment, and methods of research.

He has been married to Jackie Lynn Campbell for 37 years, and is the father of four grown children and the grandfather of eight. His hobbies are baseball, Jane Austen novels, and traveling in Scotland.

STUDENT DISCIPLINE AND CLASSROOM MANAGEMENT

Preventing and Managing Discipline Problems in the Classroom

By

JACK CAMPBELL

Mount Saint Mary's College
Emmitsburg, Maryland

Charles C Thomas
PUBLISHER • LTD.
SPRINGFIELD • ILLINOIS • U.S.A.

Published and Distributed Throughout the World by

CHARLES C THOMAS • PUBLISHER, LTD.
2600 South First Street
Springfield, Illinois 62794-9265

ISBN 0-398-07003-2 (cloth)
ISBN 0-398-07004-0 (paper)

Library of Congress Catalog Card Number: 99-37869

With THOMAS BOOKS *careful attention is given to all details of manufacturing
and design. It is the Publisher's desire to present books that are satisfactory as to their
physical qualities and artistic possibilities and appropriate for their particular use.*
THOMAS BOOKS *will be true to those laws of quality that assure a good name
and good will.*

Printed in the United States of America
CR-R-3

Library of Congress Cataloging-in-Publication Data

Campbell, Jack, Ed. D.
    Student discipline and classroom management : preventing and
managing discipline problems in the classroom / by Jack Campbell.
        p.   cm.
    Includes bibliographical references (p.   ) and index..
    ISBN 0-398-07003-2 (cloth). -- ISBN 0-398-07004-0 (paper)
    1. School discipline. 2. Classroom management. 3. Motivation in
education. I. Title.
LB3012.C34   1999
371.102'4--dc21
                                                                99-37869
                                                                CIP

This book is dedicated to Arthur F. Disque, an exemplary teacher who seldom encountered discipline problems because he was a master of student motivation and an exceptional facilitator of student self-discipline.

PREFACE

Student discipline is a major area of concern for all teachers. There is no issue about which student teachers are more concerned than discipline and classroom management. Beginning teachers tend to worry about whether students will like them, but mostly they too are concerned about discipline. Similarly, teachers early in their careers indicate that their biggest area of concern lies in discipline and classroom management. Even experienced teachers observe that their most troublesome issue is the issue of discipline in the classroom.

Order and safety in the classroom are necessary for learning to occur. Motivated students, those who willingly and persistently participate in learning activities, are orderly and tend to follow the rules and procedures that have been established. Improving the students' positive feelings and beliefs about themselves and their ability to succeed in school tends to increase the students' intrinsic motivation to learn. Understanding student self-esteem and its relationship to student motivation is invaluable in developing the appropriate plans and strategies of student discipline and classroom management. Student self-esteem must be addressed because it is directly related to student discipline.

Building student self-esteem is considerably more than simply making students feel good about themselves, and it is not something that can be addressed abstractly. Self-esteem can be improved successfully only when meaningful approbations and reinforcers are provided for legitimate success experiences in school. Similarly, understanding what student motivation is and its relationship to student discipline problems is critical. On the one hand, motivation can be seen as a construct that students have in differential amounts.

Students who have motivation do well, while unmotivated students struggle and often create discipline problems. Unfortunately, teachers frequently assume that there is nothing they can do about internal constructs such as motivation. They feel that students either have it or they don't. On the other hand, motivation can be seen as a real variable such as a form of reinforcement which is primarily external to the student. As student behavior improves as a result of reinforcers being provided, the students are often described as having improved motivation. In other words, they more willingly and persistently participate in the instructional activities that have been prepared by the teacher. Consequently, student motivation is arguably a judgment of others who have observed student behavior. Nevertheless, student motivation is unmistakenly related to student discipline.

Improving student motivation must be included in a teacher's master plan because it is so highly correlated with discipline problems in the classroom. Planning for the prevention and management of student discipline problems is one of the most important activities in which teachers must engage. A teacher's discipline strategy must be part of a total, comprehensive system of classroom management. Classroom management is proactive and includes the establishment of appropriate classroom rules and procedures. Discipline, on the other hand, is reactive and is a response to a violation of an established classroom rule or procedure. The most important objective of any system of classroom management is the prevention of discipline problems. Careful planning is the key to the prevention of discipline problems, and good planning includes carefully developed procedures and necessary and manageable classroom rules.

As teachers manage their classroom rules and procedures, they periodically encounter various kinds of student misbehaviors. If these discipline problems have not been prevented, they must be managed when they occur. There are a variety of specific strategies, ranging from non-intrusive to very intrusive, that teachers can employ to effectively deal with the myriad of discipline problems they will encounter. It is almost as though there were a "discipline staircase" teachers can climb. The higher up the stairs they go, the more intrusive become the discipline strategies. It is essential for teachers to correctly choose and effectively employ the appropriate strategy. It is important not to overreact to a situation with an intervention that is too heavy-handed, and similarly, it is necessary not to under-respond to a situation and let it get out of hand.

Whether a teacher is using a nonintrusive strategy like moving to the problem or more intrusive strategies like response-cost or time-out, the most important issue for a teacher is the issue of consistency. Whatever the rules and procedures of the class, it is imperative that the teacher respond to students in a totally consistent manner. In terms of discipline, all children must be treated exactly the same all the time. In addition to consistency, perhaps the next most important concept in student discipline is respect. If teachers are respected by their students, they will have fewer discipline problems with which to deal and will be more effective in dealing with those that occur. The first and most important step in earning students' respect is to respect them.

Even though student discipline problems can often be categorized into some general types, it is virtually impossible to anticipate particular problems and to employ predetermined strategies of intervention. Teachers need to become proficient in using a hierarchy of discipline strategies and comfortable with responding "on the spot" to a multitude of unique and unexpected situations. In order to do this effectively, it is important, if not essential, for teachers to have developed a sound theoretical foundation from which to approach each unique student discipline situation.

It is very important for teachers to understand that discipline problems are a form of student behavior. Because the misbehaviors of students are operant behaviors, they are amenable to the principles of operant conditioning or behavior management. Teachers who embrace a sound theoretical underpinning, such as behaviorism, are in an ideal position to attack the many different situations that will arise in the name of discipline problems. It is always better to respond to a discipline situation from a sound, well understood theoretical base, than it is to foolishly attempt to respond to such situations in some type of "cookbook" fashion.

This text is designed to provide that theoretical foundation and to provide a hierarchy of intervention strategies that have proven to be effective in dealing with student discipline problems. It also highlights how a theoretical foundation should be integrated into a teacher's plan of classroom management and how the hierarchy of discipline strategies form an essential component of that plan.

ACKNOWLEDGMENTS

Genuine gratitude is expressed to Nicole Bloczynski and Erica Czaja, who provided invaluable assistance with manuscript preparation. Sincere appreciation is also offered to the members of the Mount Saint Mary's College Class of 1964, whose generosity contributed significantly to the completion of this project. Finally, I offer heartfelt thanks for unqualified support and encouragement to my wife, Jackie; my children, John, Colleen, Catherine, and Kristen; and my father, Linwood Campbell.

CONTENTS

STUDENT DISCIPLINE AND CLASSROOM MANAGEMENT

Chapter 1

SELF-ESTEEM AND STUDENT MOTIVATION

S tudents with high self-esteem have a strong sense of personal efficacy. They feel good about themselves, and they are comfortable with who they are. Children who feel good about themselves tend to be motivated to succeed in school. Motivated students tend to be well behaved and to consistently follow classroom rules and procedures. They are happy, willing participants in the learning experience. They are inclined to be interested or they easily become interested in the learning activities provided by the teacher, and they tend not to disrupt or cause problems.

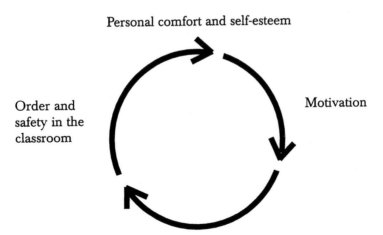

Figure 1.1. Self-esteem/motivation cycle.

A child's self-esteem is related to his motivation in school. Waschull and Kernis (1996) found that the more stable a child's self-esteem, the better they scored on measures of curiosity/interest and the more likely they were to respond to a school-related challenge. These findings relate to the cycle depicted in Figure 1.1. If a student feels good about himself and feels that he has legitimate self-worth, that student will be motivated to fully and completely participate in the teaching/learning activities of the class. Students who feel good about themselves, participating fully in the activities of the classroom, help create an orderly, safe environment for all members of the class. When students do not feel that they can be successful on the tasks of the classroom, they will tend to stop trying and before long are likely to disrupt the orderly process of the scheduled activity. In other words, they become discipline problems.

The ultimate goal, of course, is for the activities that teachers plan, organize, and implement to result in student learning. The cycle of self-esteem and student motivation can be depicted as a hierarchy which concludes with successful learning on the part of the student (Figure 1.2).

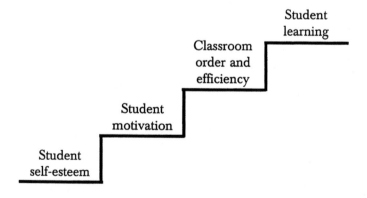

Figure 1.2. Steps to effectiveness and efficiency in the classroom.

BUILDING STUDENT SELF-ESTEEM

The more that teachers can create and maintain the self-esteem of their students, the more successful they will be in effectively facilitating student learning. Dembrowsky (1990) suggests five general ways educators can help develop self-esteem in children.

1. Develop positive teacher/student relationships.
2. Maximize the child's strengths rather than focus only on weaknesses.
3. Try to make the child's expectations more positive.
4. Help students take responsibility for their own lives.
5. Expose students to positive role models.

These are objectives with which most teachers are familiar and agree. However, they are objectives that many have not internalized or incorporated sufficiently into their teaching strategies.

Developing and Maintaining Self-esteem

Addressing the development and maintenance of the self-esteem of all students, especially those who are or might be management or discipline problems, is a primary concern of all teachers. Not only do good teachers want to create an environment where learning is occurring, they also want an environment that is orderly and safe, an environment devoid of discipline problems. An essential ingredient of such an environment is students who feel good about themselves and who are confident of their ability to be successful in school. Some specific strategies that teachers can employ to foster self-esteem in their students are:

1. *Create a sense of identity for the students.* Help them become an important component of the class and school ecology. One way to do this is to emphasize something special about each child, something at which the child is particularly good. A special identity for almost everyone can be found in such

roles as the class artist, athlete, or singer. Someone is the best reader and someone is the best at finding insects on a field trip. Everyone can have a positive identity.

2. *Form a positive teacher/student relationship.* Create an atmosphere of mutual respect; show the children that you respect them and value their efforts. Make a conscious effort to show that you care about each child in your class.

3. *Practice deliberate encouragement.* Take seriously the mandate to "catch them being good." It can certainly be at academic work, but it doesn't have to be. It can include lining up for recess, eating lunch politely, watching a film quietly, or trying really hard during math exercises. The important thing is to find legitimate reasons to praise and reinforce their achievements. Let them know that you appreciate and value their accomplishments or effort.

4. *Help them to become comfortable in learning from their mistakes.* Emphasize that it is not only acceptable to make mistakes, but it is expected. Show them how you make mistakes and learn from those mistakes.

5. *Personalize the environment for the students.* Allow students to decorate hallways and classroom bulletin boards. Display students' artwork and freely hang photographs of the students in prominent places. Help them develop responsibility for their classroom and school and encourage them to feel a sense of ownership.

6. *Help them feel that they are making a contribution to the school.* Allow each student to feel that he brings something special to the school environment and that the ambience of the class and school would be lessened without each student's unique contributions. For example, allow them to tutor younger students or to run errands for teachers.

7. *Allow them to participate in decision making to some degree.* Students cannot decide whether or not to have a test, but they can be asked when they would prefer it. Perhaps they can help determine when in the day recess should be scheduled or who should read the morning announcements. Even

minimal decision making makes them feel that they are part of the process.

8. *Help them develop the skill of self-regulation.* Responsibility is a privilege to be earned, and once it has been earned, teachers should let students know that they consider them to be responsible. Try to help students think their way through problem situations. For example, give them an opportunity to decide how much work to do each week on a long-term project.

McCracken (1995) offers similar suggestions. Specifically, she suggests that in the primary grades teachers should focus on building trust in their students by
- employing predictable schedules
- providing authentic feedback
- developing warm relationships
- showing genuine interest in each child's comments

In addition, teachers should concentrate on promoting independence in children by having them develop initial conflict resolution skills so they can attempt to resolve their own problems. McCracken (1995) concludes that teachers must encourage success and promote each child's self esteem by
- Showing genuine enthusiasm for effort and accomplishment
- Using materials which capture student interest
- Using sincere, specific, descriptive praise
- Having activities in which the students are likely to feel that they are making a real contribution

On What Is Self-esteem Based?

A child's self-esteem is dependent, in part, on the image that child has of himself. Wardle (1995) suggests that a child's self image is based on the way the environment views the child and the way the child views himself. A child who feels that he legitimately belongs to a family, a community, a culture, and a school will be in a position to develop a positive, healthy self-image. One who belongs, truly belongs, to these groups will be actively interacting with them and will be helping to formulate his own self-image. "Each child has a profound impact on the creation of his own self-image: the way he behaves and responds to the environment (Is he appropriate? fun to be around? obnoxious?) and the way he evaluates information from the environment. He is an active agent in the development of his own self-image" (Wardle, 1995, p. 44).

SELF-ESTEEM OF ATYPICAL CHILDREN

The relationship between self-esteem and motivation is well established and clearly understood by educators. Lewis (1992) points out, "It is certainly not a new idea to suggest that motivation and self-esteem are related to one another" (p. 333). The importance of developing and maintaining a student's self-esteem is paramount. Stipek's (1984) study concludes that children progressively value academic achievement as they advance through school, but their beliefs about their own academic competence and their expectations for success gradually decline. She further suggests that by age 11 children begin to believe that ability limits the effectiveness of effort.

This is especially true for exceptional children. Exceptional or underachieving children frequently develop a syndrome called *learned helplessness.* They often say things like, "I'm just not smart" or "I'm too stupid to do this." They conclude that regardless of what they do, they just will not be successful in school. They come to believe that they are helpless in terms of achieving academic success. Dev (1996) points out that learning disabled students have a tendency to attribute their successes or failures to external factors such as luck or other people. Dev goes on to conclude that teaching learning disabled students to attribute performance outcomes to their own efforts rather than external factors can improve their intrinsic motivation. It is easy to understand that any kind of prolonged history of believing that they will not be successful, will certainly affect children's self-esteem and consequently their motivation.

Disabled Readers

Exceptional children and many children who are considered typical frequently manifest learning problems in a variety of academic areas. Reading is overwhelmingly the academic area in which teachers see the most frequent learning problems. In discussing strategies for working with disabled readers, Castle (1994) offers seven guidelines for teachers for building supportive learning environments. Such supportive learning environments will tend to facilitate the development of student self-esteem.

1. Believe in the possibility and probability of success. Teachers must be sure they are conveying the assumption that children will be able to improve.

2. Try to create peer acceptance. Children often consider peers to be significant influences in their lives. Try to foster positive peer interactions and a climate where all are valued as individuals.

3. Put reading success in proper perspective. The inability to read effectively does not mean an inability to learn. Demonstrate that the ability to read is not the only means whereby students can gain recognition.

4. Capitalize on student interests. Build instruction around high interest material that may well serve as a motivator for achievement and positive attitudes.

5. Focus on how reading communicates. For example, be careful not to damage self-perception by demanding oral reading prior to purposeful silent reading or by insisting on

perfect grammar and punctuation in a writing assignment without allowing first drafts to capture essential ideas. Also be sure students have sufficient background information on a topic before requiring them to read about it.

6. Expand the positive environment beyond the classroom. In trying to improve a student's self-esteem, teachers must always include a conscious attempt to affect the home environment. Try to include parents in the task of building self-esteem in their children.

7. Be a role model. Students will learn as much in terms of attitudes and behaviors from what they see teachers doing as from what they hear them saying. Help them understand that reading provides information to you. Let them see that you enjoy reading and that it makes you feel good.

Minority Students

In addressing the development of self-esteem, substantial consideration must also be given to the unique circumstances and characteristics of minority students. "Studies on minority children have yielded mixed results concerning relationships between components of intrinsic motivation and self-perceptions, and achievement" (p. 84).

Marchant (1991) conducted a study of self-esteem and motivation of forty-seven African American urban students. His major findings were:

- Many were reliant on the teacher for evaluations of success and failure.
- General feelings of self-worth and happiness were not related to their perceptions of their behavioral conduct or their scholastic competence. Instead, physical appearance and athletic ability seemed to be more important to these students sense of self-worth.
- Although pursuing challenging activities may be related to more positive feelings about school learning, it may be perceived as socially unacceptable.

• Students who had better perceptions of their scholastic ability had better attendance than those who had lower perceptions of academic competence.

Self-concept of academic ability depends in large measure on the child's self-comparison to relevant others. Children in lower achieving homogeneous groups assess themselves higher than they would in more heterogeneous groups. Teachers need to be creative in finding ways to assist minority children in making comparisons with appropriate peers. School guidance counselors can be an invaluable resource in such situations. "Classroom guidance activities provide an excellent forum for promoting motivation in the classroom on the part of all students, while also helping to advance self-esteem" (Lewis, 1992, p. 337).

Although the results of Marchant's (1991) study are far from generalizable to all black urban elementary students, the following represent some possible practical implications of this study:

1. Black urban elementary students may require extra efforts to promote self-regulation in their learning. Teachers need to help students establish their own goals and to guide students in ways that encourage self-monitoring of success.

2. Black urban elementary students may need early encouragement and specific examples that highlight the relevance of doing well in school. Teachers should present the "why" of learning along with the "what" and "how."

3. Black urban elementary students may not find the pursuit of challenging work socially desirable. Teachers need to find ways to reward motivated students in a manner which encourages socialization.

4. Black urban elementary students who trust their own judgments but do not perceive themselves as being scholastically competent may have more attendance problems. Since this relationship is likely to play an increasing role in attendance and achievement as the student matures, teachers need to find a way to provide students with choices the students can succeed at in school.

5. Black urban elementary students may find improving their standard English vocabulary socially undesirable. Teachers and communities need to find ways to encourage and reward the practice of learning English vocabulary in order to facilitate communication in school and outside a restricted urban area.

6. Black urban elementary students may rely on the performance and value systems of their peers in order to evaluate their own performance and self-worth. Teachers need to strive for academic standards and educational values that are not dependent upon a small racial cultural reference group. At the same time, teachers need to be aware of and respect local belief systems.

7. Black urban elementary students must be shown that they can succeed in school and in life. The rewards of "real" achievement will lead to a more positive, more complete self concept. Nothing succeeds like success (Marchant, 1991, p. 98).

REALISTIC SELF-ESTEEM DEVELOPMENT

It would be fair to observe that teachers are continually deluged with reminders about their responsibility to develop and enhance the self-esteem of their students. McGerald and Nidds (1996) somewhat humorously suggest that the underlying assumption is that low self-esteem is at the root of *all* student problems and is the root cause of children's unhappiness, depression, weight disorders, delinquency, and learning problems. Self-esteem, happiness, and comfort of students have become objectives unto themselves. Considerable effort is often extended to facilitate students' enjoyment of a learning activity. It is almost the case that we have become more concerned with our students "liking" reading than with their becoming "good" at reading. Teachers are frequently pressed to help children feel generically good about themselves rather than to feel good about their successes. They are becoming increasingly reluctant to say anything negative about students for fear of damaging their self-esteem. This well intended, but misguided, practice must be abandoned.

William Damon (1991) tells the story of his son in kindergarten who came home from school early in the year with a 3 x 5 index card on which was written, "I'm terrific." His son explained that every child in the class was given a similar card and asked to recite the words every day. When asked to explain, his son said that he was terrific and that his friends were terrific. The boy went on to respond that he had no idea about why, how, or what they were terrific at. Damon persuasively explains that such self-esteem boosting is fruitless and that self-esteem is not a virtue that can be transmitted abstractly. "We would do better to help children acquire the skills, values, and virtues on which a positive sense of self is properly built" (Damon, 1991, p. 12). Praise and affirmation for such skills, values, and virtues would then be highly appropriate. Affirming communications must be embedded in concrete statements about actual personal qualities, abilities, or actions if they are to have any impact.

Generic self-esteem boosting is not valuable, nor is it the way to effectively develop self-esteem in students. Academic challenges and achievements in school are legitimate ways to enhance self-worth, self-confidence, and acceptance by one's peers (i.e., self-esteem). Children will develop appropriate self-esteem as they experience success in the school-related activities teachers provide for them. Needless to say, teachers must assure that the activities to which they expose children will result in success experiences for them. "With each accomplishment, students gain self-confidence, which in turn generates intrinsic motivation, the source of long term dedication that enables students to master complex concepts and difficult subject matter" (McGerald & Nidds, 1996, p. 55).

Teachers must build student self-esteem on the real success experiences children have in school. The experiences cannot be made to seem successful if they are not. If a student says the capital of Nevada is Reno, no amount of finessing will make that response correct. He can be complimented for trying, but there is nothing wrong with telling him that his answer is wrong. Self-esteem is built on the girders of confidence, which in turn is built on the strong foundation of legitimate success experiences.

If students experience legitimate success experiences in school, they will most assuredly increase their levels of confidence about learning activities and other school-related situations. As their confidence grows and develops, there will inevitably be a corresponding increase in their self esteem. Confident students with appropriate levels of self-esteem tend to be seen as *motivated* students or students who have *intrinsic motivation*, and they tend not to cause discipline problems.

REFERENCES

Castle, M.: Promoting the disabled reader's self-esteem. *Reading and Writing Quarterly: Overcoming Learning Disabilities, 10*(2), 159–170, 1994.

Damon, William: Putting substance into self-esteem: A focus on academic and moral values. *Educational Horizons, 70*(1), 36–40, 1991.

Dembrowsky, C. H.: Developing self-steem and internal motivation in at-risk youth. Paper presented at National Council for Self-Esteem, Orlando, FL, March 23, 1990, ED332130, 1990.

Lewis, A. C.: Student motivation and learning: The role of the school counselor. *The School Counselor, 39*(5), 333–337, 1992.

Marchant, G. J.: A profile of motivation, self-perception, and achievement in black urban elementary students. *The Urban Review, 23*(2), 83–99, 1991.

McCracken, J. B.: Image-building: Hands-on developmental process. *Child Care Information Exchange, 7*, 48–55, 1995.

McGerald, J., and Nidds, J. A.: (Self-esteem or self-confidence? *Principal, 76*(1), 55, 1996.

Owens, T. J., Mortimer, J. T., and Finch, M. D.: Self-determination as a source of self-esteem in adolescence. *Social Forces, 74*(4), 1377–1404, 1996.

Waschull, S. B., and Kernis, M. H.: Level and stability of self-esteem as predictors of children's intrinsic motivation and reasons for anger. *Personality and Social Psychology Bulletin, 22*(1), 4–13, 1996.

Wardle, F.: How young children build images of themselves. *Child Care Information Exchange,* July (104), 44–47, 1995.

Chapter 2

MOTIVATION

W e are relatively comfortable describing motivated students. They are happy, willing, even eager participants in the learning process. They tend to be interested, or they easily become interested in the instructional activities the teacher has prepared. Motivated students choose working partners according to skill and ability and not according to popularity or friendship. Motivated students persist longer at a task than unmotivated students, and they perform equally well with or without supervision. They choose larger, future rewards as opposed to more immediate gratification. Because they enthusiastically, willingly, and responsibly participate in instructional activities, motivated students tend not to cause discipline problems.

WHAT IS MOTIVATION?

Defining motivation, however, becomes a bit more tricky. A major theory used to define or explain motivation was developed by Abraham Maslow, and it is often referred to as Maslow's *hierarchy of needs* theory. This theory suggests that initially, basic deficiency needs of survival, safety, belonging, and self-esteem must be met. After these deficiency needs have been met, the student focuses on growth needs of knowledge, beauty, and self-actualization. Although it is unarguable that a starving child or a child in mortal fear for her life will not be giving priority to a science lesson, the entire concept of needs reduction is not universally accepted.

(Maslow's theory of motivation will be addressed further in Chapter 3.)

In fact, the entire concept of motivation is open to serious debate. Many see motivation as a valid variable with which they can work. Others see motivation as a *hypothetical construct* based on the observable behaviors children emit. However it is approached, motivation is a term which cries out for an operational definition. However, before we construct a workable operational definition of motivation, it will be worthwhile to consider some practical approaches to this concept.

APPROACHES TO MOTIVATION

Student motivation can be approached from a variety of perspectives including the humanistic approach of Maslow. Motivation can also be viewed from a cognitive approach, a social learning point of view or a behavioral perspective. What follows will be an attempt to address two pragmatic considerations of motivation and to integrate the two in a meaningful, practical way.

General and Specific Motivation

" . . . [s]tudent *motivation to learn* can be conceptualized either as a general trait or as a situation-specific state" (Brophy, 1987b, p. 40).

General motivation to learn or to participate in learning activities is a broad, general disposition which is enduring in nature. It can be seen as a student's desire to strive for knowledge and skill mastery in school-related situations. The enduring nature of general motivation is critical because once it is developed, general motivation persists. The broadness is also an important feature because motivation cuts across all aspects of the school curriculum. General motivation is the result of a long history of experiences with teachers, classrooms, and schools. It is thought to be a construct that resides within the learner.

On the other hand, the source of *specific motivation* is seen as the topic or the teacher, and a child's specific motivation depends in large measure on the skill and enthusiasm of the teacher. It tends to be unstable over time and tends to fluctuate with the changing of topics and lessons.

> As a general *trait*, motivation to learn refers to an enduring disposition to value learning as a worthwhile and satisfying activity, and thus to strive for knowledge and mastery in learning situations. . . . In specific situations, a *state* of motivation to learn exists when task engagement is guided by the goal or intention of acquiring the knowledge or mastering the skill that the task is designed to teach. (Brophy, 1987a, pp. 181–182).

Specific motivation energizes students for a particular lesson or activity. Even the most obstreperous and recalcitrant students actively participate in classroom activities that they enjoy or find interesting. Because learning disabled students tend not to attribute their successes and failures to their own ability and effort, they depend more than most on the teacher for motivation. (Dev, 1996). One could easily conceive of the goal of using specific motivation to develop general motivation.

The goal, of course, is to have or develop students with abundant amounts of general motivation. The question becomes one of how to develop general motivation in students who apparently do not have any.

Extrinsic and Intrinsic Motivation

A behaviorally oriented person might see motivation as reinforcement. It has been well established that reinforced behavior occurs more frequently than behavior that is not reinforced. Given that a student will have to engage in some behavior in order for teachers to make a judgment about whether the child is or is not motivated, it is possible to manipulate the consequences of student behavior to create motivation. This type of motivation is known as *extrinsic motivation*. As an example, it is easy to see how reinforcement in the form of high test scores, improved grades, teacher compliments, or peer acceptance can be very motivating.

On the other hand, *intrinsic motivation* is often viewed as a response to needs such as curiosity or persistence that exist within the learner. Teachers often refer to such students as having a "love of learning" or as enjoying learning "for its own sake." They are implying that there is some internal force or construct that some students have that drives them to work hard, be interested, and stay on task. Intuitively most teachers would prefer that their students be intrinsically motivated.

In looking at the concepts of extrinsic and intrinsic motivation more closely, we can see that intrinsic motivation is much the same thing as self-control. ". . . [w]e call it self-control only when the individual seeks to increase the strength of behavior that is considered desirable by members of his society or to decrease the strength of behavior that is considered undesirable" (Reese, 1966, p. 48). All of us who have developed some degree of self-control have had a series of specific behaviors consistently reinforced throughout our lives. In other words we received some form of extrinsic motivation (i.e., encouragement, praise, money, or cookies) for behaviors over which we ultimately began to exercise self-control (i.e., studying, partying, or praying). The more an individual is successful in developing self-control, the more it can be said that she is developing intrinsic motivation. Feelings of self-determination and intrinsic motivation could well be reciprocal ". . . with intrinsic motivation influencing self-esteem and self-esteem influencing intrinsic motivation, in a dynamic ongoing process" (Owens et al., 1996, p. 1388).

IMPROVING MOTIVATION

Those who hold that motivation is a real, viable variable that is internal and something that a student has or does not have, typically experience genuine difficulty when faced with the task of attempting to increase a student's motivation. Some teachers won't even try, claiming that motivation is something you are born with and that interventions are fruitless when faced with an "unmotivated child." Others may attempt some environmental restructuring, but feel that their efforts will depend in large measure on the child's success in developing an increase in the amount of "internal motivation." Some teachers, however, begin using extrinsic motivation (reinforcement) to establish and maintain authentic success experiences for the child. Their purpose, of course, is to help the child develop a sense of intrinsic motivation. In other words, they are attempting to *teach* motivation.

It turns out that motivation can be taught. Hilker (1993) conducted a study at the University of Virginia whose purpose was, among other things, to determine if students' motivational orientations can be changed. Initially, she administered an accepted self-report survey that employed a scale of intrinsic vs. extrinsic orientation to two groups of sixth grade students. The students ranked themselves along a continuum of being intrinsically or extrinsically motivated. She then taught a two-week social studies unit to the two groups. For one group, she used intrinsic motivators such as helping students set resourceful goals, having students monitor and reinforce themselves, and having students choose an appropriate final project to demonstrate learning. For the second group, extrinsic motivators, primarily a token system, was employed. At the end of the two-week unit the survey was re-administered.

Findings indicate that a student's motivational orientations can be changed when exposed over time to an environment with a particular motivational orientation. She cautions, how-

ever, against assuming that it is appropriate to work only on the development of intrinsic motivation. "To use a motivational system which incorporates only intrinsic motivators assumes that schools will provide students opportunities to learn only what is interesting to them and that schools will not demand that students learn those things which do not interest them. This is neither reasonable nor wise. . ." (Hilker, 1993, p. 51). The use of extrinsic motivation, or said another way, the use of reinforcement is both proper and effective when exposing students to lessons they do not find inherently interesting. This is indeed an appropriate strategy for the development of specific motivation.

The more involved a student is in the activities of instruction and the learning process, the less likely that student is to be involved in any kind of disciplinary problem. The degree of involvement with the task or the degree to which a new concept or new material is understandable to a student depends, in large measure, on the depth of processing in which she engages. The more that a student is motivated, the more likely she is to actively engage the learning process. According to Pintrich et al. (1993), the depth of processing is related to motivational factors such as whether she has more of a mastery (focus on learning) or a performance (focus on a grade or competition) orientation. It is also related to her level of interest and her belief about her ability to be successful. Similarly, according to Cordova and Lepper (1996) the results of their study indicate that students who were motivated became more deeply involved in the activities, attempted more complex operations, and consequently learned more. They point out that student motivation can be enhanced when teachers make an effort to personalize the curriculum to some degree by including individualized information about the student's background and interests. Motivation is also enhanced by providing the students a reasonable amount of choice. "Likewise, students who were offered a modicum of choice over instructionally incidental aspects of the learning contexts showed greater increases in motivation and learning" (Cordova & Lepper, 1996, p. 726).

REINFORCEMENT AS EXTRINSIC MOTIVATION

If a student will not participate in a learning activity, it is not uncommon for a teacher to declare that the student is not motivated. This is especially true if the student has a long history of reluctance to participate. However, if the student is reinforced properly for approximations of the desired behavior or for executing the desired behavior, it is extremely likely that the student will participate more frequently and more willingly. As a student participates more willingly, resulting in a claim that she is becoming more motivated. The claim for increased motivation becomes even stronger if the new behavior maintains over time.

For example, if Colleen, a sixth grade student, refuses to participate in mathematics lessons and in fact often "acts out" during mathematics, her teacher might well declare that she is an "unmotivated student." Colleen's lack of interest and visible unhappiness during mathematics would only support the claim of lack of motivation. However, if the teacher began to reinforce her with opportunities to listen to favorite CDs for any attempts to participate in mathematics, Colleen's participation in mathematics would most likely increase. The more she experienced success (resulting in appropriate external reinforcement), the happier and more willing she would become. A shrewd teacher will naturally stretch the schedule of reinforcement and accompany the external or primary reinforcers with secondary reinforcers like praise statements, pats on the back, and genuine looks of approval. Praise is a powerful reinforcer, but it is crucial to be sincere in delivering praise and to only deliver praise when the student's behavior warrants it. Grey (1995) points out that praise is often *empty* and does not consider the child's reality. She maintains that empty praise doesn't tell the child what is being affirmed or why you think it is good. Teacher and parental praise statements should have validity and be linked to real effort and achievement. "They . . . must encourage children to develop specific skills and values" (Damon, 1991, p. 14). In our previous example genuine praise and other nonverbal affirmations should be tied directly to Colleen's behavior. In time, the primary reinforcers would be essentially replaced with secondary reinforcers resulting in Colleen's ecology providing the same type of reinforcement that it does to "motivated" students. This scenario might well result in the teacher stating that Colleen's motivation had increased.

It is easy to see why some strongly suggest that motivation is only a hypothetical construct. Claims that Colleen's improved behavior was the result of increased motivation can more easily and more accurately be explained as resulting from external reinforcement. Because they come from outside the learner, reinforcers are potential extrinsic motivators. As success experiences accumulate another type of consequence may serve as a motivator. Colleen may want to avoid the consequences of failing the test or not completing the homework. "Prior school grades also enhance intrinsic motivation at school" (Owens et al., 1996, p. 1396). The more effective the external reinforcers are, the more success Colleen will experience. The more success she has, the more likely that she will develop a desire to continue doing well, that is, to experience intrinsic motivation.

There exists in the literature some criticisms of the use of rewards and the suggestion that rewards actually decrease intrinsic motivation (Lepper et al., 1996; Ryan & Deci, 1996; Kohn, 1996). This is actually not the case at all, and Cameron and Pierce (1996) establish that rewards can be used effectively to enhance a student's intrinsic interest in activities. Responding to their critics Cameron and Pierce (1996) strongly maintain that their work has documented that verbal praise and performance feedback increase the value of an activity. "When tangible rewards are offered contingent on level of performance or are given unexpectedly, students remain motivated in the subject area" (p. 40). They do acknowledge that a slight negative effect can be expected when a teacher gives a tangible reward without regard to the student's performance; however, good teachers wouldn't provide reinforcement in such a manner.

If a student has a history of being reinforced properly for effort *and* performance on a wide range of school tasks, it is likely that she will develop general motivation.

DEVELOPING STUDENT MOTIVATION

Developing student motivation is a difficult task for most teachers. Nevertheless, it is an important objective because when successful, students will perform better academically and will tend not to cause or contribute to discipline problems in the classroom. According to Owens et al. (1996), students with high grades come to find schoolwork more meaningful and interesting and feel they are improving their ability to think and solve problems. They further indicate that teachers, in trying to develop student motivation, tend to respond to student performance, and they go on to point out that a student's intrinsic motivation for schoolwork is not affected by the social class of the parents or the student's innate ability.

Eggen and Kauchak (1997) provide a superb explanation of how to develop and support student motivation. The two major suggestions that they offer are:
1. Promote a climate of cooperation rather than competition.
2. Focus on improvement rather than ability.

According to Eggen and Kauchak (1997) three critical variables must be working in harmony in order to accomplish these suggestions.

The first of these variables is *teacher characteristics* or the teacher's personal orientation toward students, teaching, and learning. Nothing is as important to developing student motivation as the teacher characteristics of modeling, enthusiasm, warmth and empathy, and positive expectations.

- Teacher modeling–teachers must model genuine enthusiasm and interest.
- Teacher enthusiasm–teachers must consciously demonstrate both verbally and nonverbally their enthusiasm for the activity.
- Teacher warmth and empathy–teachers must demonstrate that teaching is a human activity of relating effectively with people.
- Teacher expectations–teachers must communicate their belief that students can be successful.

The second variable is classroom climate or the characteristics of the classroom that promote feelings of security, understanding, and appropriate challenge. The steps to creating an appropriate classroom climate are:

1. Keep order and safety in the classroom.
2. Cultivate a climate of success and satisfaction.
3. Assure comprehension and understanding.
4. Maintain a level of appropriate challenge.

An important element in the total classroom climate is the issue of competition. The question of competition and its effect on student motivation and performance is interesting. Almost all teachers have employed some form of competition (spelling bees, contests, games), and many also have stressed that they want their students to compete only with themselves and not with other students. Some feel competition builds character and confidence while others feel it makes students insecure and unwilling to participate. Tripathi (1992) reports that direct competition with another student and some type of controlling information provided by the teacher lead to improved immediate performance. However, competition against a standard and feedback about competence results in greater intrinsic motivation.

The third crucial variable according to Eggen and Kauchak (1997) is *instructional variables.* Student motivation and particularly specific motivation is often dependent on the lesson and the materials used in the lesson. "In particular, the state of motivation to learn exists when students engage in classroom tasks with the goal of understanding the content and activate strategies for developing such understanding. Further, the trait or generalized disposition of motivation to learn exists when students routinely seek to accomplish the intended academic goals, either because they enjoy and take satisfaction in learning or because they feel duty-bound to do so" (Lee & Brophy, 1996, pp. 304–305).

If students are to be successful and remain on task, it is essential that they attend to and become involved in the lesson. After attracting a student's attention the teacher must attempt to personalize it for her and then to involve her in the lesson. The student should receive constant feedback on her performance and sincere praise for her efforts and successes.

The issue of student motivation is also addressed by Lumsden (1994) who summarizes some strategies for fostering motivation. In her comprehensive review she reports that Brophy (1986) offers four basic types of strategies that teachers can use.

1. *Maintain students' expectations of success.* Emphasize persistence, mastery, and progress.

2. *Supply extrinsic motivation.* Use things that students value, such as good grades, rewards, or special privileges. Be careful not to allow students to become overly reliant on them.

3. *Capitalize on existing intrinsic motivation.* Provide students an opportunity to respond and to receive feedback from you and their peers.

4. *Stimulate student motivation to learn.* Model interest in and enthusiasm for learning.

She goes on to point out that Raffini (1993) suggests similar but subtly different strategies, including:

- Assess student's interests, hobbies, and extracurricular activities.
- Occasionally present information and argue positions contrary to student assumptions.
- Use divergent questions and brainstorming activities.

These are but a few of the good ideas teachers have and can use to foster motivation in their students.

The importance of specific classroom activities to develop and support student motivation is clear. It is also clear that the more student motivation is developed, the fewer the number of discipline problems a teacher will have to confront. However, there is not an abundance of research in the area of students' intrinsic motivation. Only recently are we becoming aware of the important contribution classroom teachers can make in helping to formulate effective and efficient strategies for fostering student motivation. Future research in this area perhaps should focus on cooperative efforts between researchers and classroom teachers. "Researchers working collaboratively with teachers should be able to develop a richer understanding of the dynamics of student motivation and teacher action in the classroom" (Nolen & Nicholls, 1993, p. 67).

SUSTAINING MOTIVATION

Many children come to school exhibiting behavior that most teachers would agree indicates adequate levels of motivation. Frequently, children for whom that could not be said develop what is considered to be increased levels of motivation. For these reasons it is important to consider factors which sustain motivation over time. Story and Sullivan (1986) indicate that the most common measure of continuing motivation is whether students return to the same task at a later time. In their study they provide a summary of key factors influencing a student's decision to return to a task. These factors are:

- Feedback from teachers regarding success or competence.
- High levels of performance on the initial task.
- The students' own perception of their performance; the better they think they performed, the more likely they are to return to that task.
- The difficulty level of the task; it cannot be too difficult.
- How interesting the task was to the students.

The factors that influence continuing motivation which were determined or substantiated in Story and Sullivan (1986) provide important implications for classroom practice. For example, when a task is too difficult for a student, the teacher should break it down into smaller, easier component tasks for her. Similarly, teachers should provide students ample opportunity to practice the skills they are developing so that they build up appropriate levels of confidence. Perhaps most importantly, teachers must make every attempt to make their teaching activities as interesting to the students as possible. Sometimes this can be accomplished by employing appropriate media or by creating competitive games as part of the lesson.

The issue of sustaining motivation takes on a special importance when the issue of more able or gifted children is considered. The motivation of these children was highlighted in a study by Vallerand et al. (1994). In this study, 64 boys and 71 girls were assessed on measures of extrinsic/intrinsic orientation and cognitive perceived competence. Of the 135 students (average CA= 10.1) used in this study, 69 were identified as gifted and 66 were enrolled in regular elementary classes. It is important to note that the gifted students used in this study were enrolled in homogeneous, self-contained classes.

Vallerand et al. (1994) defined intrinsic motivation as a student's willingness to participate voluntarily in an activity in the absence of rewards or punishment. They also point out that intrinsic motivation is increased when students engage in activities that are likely to provide them feelings of competence and freedom.

The results of this study revealed two very important findings:

- Gifted students displayed higher levels of intrinsic motivation than students in regular classes.
- Gifted students perceived themselves to be more cognitively competent than regular students.

Because the gifted students in this study were enrolled in homogeneous classes, they had the opportunity to explore, learn new things, and exchange ideas among students of similar intellectual skills at their own accelerated pace. In fact

> . . . it could be hypothesized that the intrinsic motivation of gifted students might be diminished in the context of heter-ogeneous classes because these students would have to progress at the (slower) pace of the regular students. Indeed, the fact of being told repeatedly to be quiet and give other students a chance to express themselves might be sufficient to undermine gifted students' sense of freedom and consequently their intrinsic motivation. Gifted students in such instances would not feel competent but rather controlled by the classroom and would not experience intrinsic motivation. (Vallerand et al., 1994, p. 174)

Another important issue concerning the motivation of gifted children is its stability. This issue was examined by Gottfried and Gottfried (1996) when they assessed 107 children with the Wechsler Intelligence Scale for Children-Revised (WISC-R) for the purpose of determining giftedness. Those in the sample with full scale IQ scores of 130 or higher were identified as gifted.

Academic intrinsic motivation of the sample was assessed at ages 9, 10, and 13 with the Children's Academic Intrinsic Motivation Inventory. Although there was no significant main effect for gender, it was found that the difference in intrinsic motivation between gifted children and the comparison group remained stable over time. "Relative to the comparison group children, those who were identified as gifted at age 8 evidenced superior academic intrinsic motivation at ages 9 through 13 years across academic subject areas and for school in general" (Gottfried & Gottfried, 1996, p. 181).

In order to sustain the intrinsic motivation of more able or gifted students, especially those in heterogeneous settings, it is important that they be presented with challenging learning environments that will allow them to test their abilities and to develop perceptions of their competence. It is also important that they continue to receive positive feedback to support the development and maintenance of intrinsic motivation.

Motivation Defined

If motivation is not defined as some form of reinforcement, it is usually defined as some type of internal construct. Because such internal constructs are impossible to validate, they are usually based on the observable behavior of the student. Typically, someone observes the behavior and declares the student to be motivated to a greater or lesser degree.

Consequently, we can define motivation as follows:

Student motivation is the perception others (i.e., teachers) have concerning the willingness, enthusiasm, and persistence of a student's on-task behavior. It includes the student's level of self-control of that behavior and the perception of the student and others concerning the intrinsic nature of that behavior.

REFERENCES

Brophy, J.: Socializing students' motivation to learn. In M. L. Maehr and D. A. Kleiber (Eds.), *Advances in Motivation and Achievement* (Vol. 5), (pp. 181–210). Greenwich, CT, JAI Press, 1987a.

Brophy, J.: Synthesis of research on strategies for motivating students to learn. *Educational Leadership, 45* (2), 40–48, 1987b.

Cameron, J., and Pierce, W. D.: The debate about rewards and intrinsic motivation: Protests and accusations do not alter the results. *Review of Educational Research, 66*(1), 39–51, 1996.

Cordova, D. I. and Lepper, M. R.: Intrinsic motivation and the process of learning: Beneficial effects of contextualization, personalization, and choice. *Journal of Educational Psychology, 88*(4), 715–730, 1996.

Damon, W:. Putting substance into self-esteem: A focus on academic and moral values. *Educational Horizons, 70*(1), 36–40, 1991.

Dev, P. C.: Intrinsic motivation and the student with learning disabilities. 2–31, 1996.

Grey, K.: Not in praise of praise. *Exchange, 104*, 56–59, 1995.

Gottfried, A. E., and Gottfried, A. W: A longitudinal study of academic intrinsic motivation in intellectually gifted children: Childhood through early adolescence. *Gifted Child Quarterly, 40*(4), 179–183, 1996.

Hilker, J. B.: Toward creating the intrinsically motivating classroom: Can students motivational orientations be changed? 2–84, 1993.

Kohn, A.: By all available means: Cameron and Pierce's defense of extrinsic motivators. *Review of Educational Research, 66*, 1–4, 1996.

Lee, O., and Brophy, J.: Motivational patterns observed in sixth-grade science classrooms. *Journal of Research in Science Teaching, 33*(3), 303–318, 1996.

Lepper, M. R., Keavney, M., and Drake, M.: Intrinsic motivation and extrinsic rewards: A commentary on Cameron and Pierce's meta-analysis. *Review of Educational Research, 66*, 5–32, 1996.

Lumsden, L. S.: Student motivation. *Research Roundup, 10*(3), 2–5, 1994.

Nolen, S. B., and Nicholls, J. G.: A place to begin (again) in research on student motivation: Teachers' beliefs. *Teaching and Teacher Education, 10*(1), 57–69, 1994.

Pintrich, P. R., Marx, R. W., and Boyle, R. A.: Beyond cold conceptual change: The role of motivational beliefs and classroom contextual factors in the process of conceptual change. *Review of Educational Research, 63*(2), 167–199, 1993.

Ryan, R. M., and Deci, E. L.: When paradigms clash: Comments on Cameron and Pierce's claim that rewards do not undermine intrinsic motivation. *Review of Educational Research, 66*, 33-38, 1996.

Story, N. O., and Sullivan, H. J.: Factors that influence continuing motivation. *Journal of Educational Research, 80*(2), 86–92, 1986.

Tripathi, K. N.: Competition and intrinsic motivation. *Journal of Social Psychology, 132*(6), 709–715, 1992.

Vallerand, R. J., Gagne, F., Senecal, C., and Pelletier, L. G.: A comparison of the school intrinsic motivation and perceived competence of gifted and regular students. *Gifted Child Quarterly, 38*(4), 172–175, 1994.

Chapter 3

THE CONNECTION BETWEEN MOTIVATION AND MISBEHAVIOR

JACK CAMPBELL AND TAMARA HATCH

It is not uncommon for teachers to talk freely about discipline problems they have encountered and to discuss such cases openly with their colleagues. However, when asked to define *discipline problem*, they frequently have some difficulty pinning it down. Responding to this problem, an article was published (McDaniel, 1981) where students were characterized as representing various "types" of discipline problems. They were labeled with general, descriptive terms like *clown, bully, baby, sneak, smart-aleck, cheat,* and blasé. These were familiar terms to most teachers because most teachers have had students, at one time or another, who behaved in such a way as to be characterized as a *bully* or as a *clown*, etc., and these students often would be identified as discipline problems.

In reality there are an extraordinary number of types of discipline problems with which teachers have to deal. In attempting to identify what constitutes discipline problems, McDaniel (1981) states, ". . . it is probably better to think of students' discipline problems in terms of the effect of their behavior on *their* learning and social growth rather than on your teaching and peace of mind" (p. 225). In other words, a discipline problem is a student whose behavior inhibits his learning or the learning of other students. McDaniel goes on to point out that most teachers would readily characterize the *bully* or the *smart-aleck* as a discipline problem, but they should be equally concerned about the *brown-noser* or the

32

sleeper. In one way or another, they all lack self-discipline and need to be helped to change their motivations and behavioral styles. Without a change in motivation, such children will experience genuine difficulty in accomplishing their learning objectives.

One of the most common complaints of teachers is that students lack motivation. Some educators would suggest that students always are motivated by various needs and desires, but in many cases, the motivation results in misbehavior, not learning behavior. Misbehavior often occurs because the student is motivated to satisfy needs more basic than learning (Maslow, 1954; Wlodkowski, 1986). For a student who feels incompetent or rejected in school, misbehavior provides intrinsic rewards greater than the rewards provided by on-task, learning-oriented behavior (Adelman & Taylor, 1990; Heavey et al., 1989). The key to motivating a student to engage in positive, learning-oriented behavior is first to examine the classroom environment and the needs and interests of the particular student. The next step is to work with the student in devising new activities or learning conditions that will be more intrinsically rewarding than the results of misbehavior (Adelman & Taylor, 1990; Klausmeier & Ghatala, 1971). There are many theories of motivation and many techniques for increasing motivation, but one theme that seems to run through all of them is that students are most motivated to learn and behave appropriately when they feel they have some control over the learning situation.

MASLOW'S EXPLANATION OF MOTIVATION

There are a host of theoretical constructs that examine motivation and its effect on behavior, but one of the most popular and helpful might be the hierarchy proposed by psychologist Abraham Maslow. Maslow (1954) theorized that human behavior is motivated by a hierarchy of needs. The most basic are physiological needs that must be at least partially fulfilled before higher needs can be met. For example, there is the need for food. A person who is hungry will be most motivated to obtain food, not to fulfill some higher need. When the physiological needs are satisfied, a set of higher needs emerges: the safety needs, such as the need for security, stability, and law and order. When those needs are at least partially fulfilled, there emerges the need for love and belonging; then the need for esteem, such as the desire to feel accepted emerges. Maslow also identified cognitive needs for knowledge and understanding, and aesthetic needs to appreciate life and beauty. Finally, there is the need for self-actualization, to do what best fulfills the individual.

It is easy to see how Maslow's hierarchy might apply to the classroom. Wlodkowski (1986) stated that students who are busy trying to satisfy any of the lower needs will not devote their full attention to learning and may instead engage in off-task or disruptive behavior. For example, in the physiological realm, are the students hungry? Are they too warm? Concerning the issue of safety, do they feel threatened or intimidated? In terms of students' self-esteem needs, are they concentrating on becoming liked by their peers instead of paying attention to schoolwork? Does the class structure thwart them in their efforts to do what it is they like to do? Problems will inevitably arise if students are primarily motivated by a desire to fulfill basic needs. "Unless the basic needs are met, learning becomes a difficult task because the student's energy is devoted to coping with the pain and state of deprivation his/her body is feeling" (Wlodkowski, 1986, p. 64). Wlodkowski gave many suggestions for satisfying students' needs in all of Maslow's identified areas. For example, he noted that sleepy students can be crabby or hungry and bored students tend to be restless. When students experience these feelings, they are motivated to alleviate them. "Misbehavior is more stimulating and can allow for a diversion to avoid feeling thirsty, uncomfortable, etc."

(Wlodkowski, 1986, p. 64). Wlodkowski recommended that teachers not reprimand students for being restless or inattentive, but instead indicate that they see the students are restless and ask them what might be done about it. Students who are hungry might need a snack; those who are restless might need to stretch. Students who do not feel accepted by classmates might benefit from being in a classroom in which duties and responsibilities are divided up among everyone in the class.

In regard to Maslow's highest level, self-actualization, students who are not given the opportunity to realize their full potential in the learning situation may become disinterested and disruptive. Wlodkowski suggests that teachers involve students in deciding what they will learn by, for example, allowing them to choose from a range of learning styles and topics that appeal to them. He also recommends that teachers encourage creativity, provide opportunities for problem solving and academic risk-taking, and allow students, when feasible, to figure out their own ways to do things. It is clear that many of these strategies share a common theme: they make a student responsible for his own learning. A key impediment to motivation, and a major cause of misbehavior, is when students feel they do not exercise at least some control of their situations.

PERCEIVED CONTROL AND MOTIVATION

Regardless of the particular theory of motivation, it seems the common thread running through all the professional literature is that people are most motivated to achieve when they believe they have some control over their own lives. In the classroom, students who feel others are excessively controlling them often exhibit behavior problems. When junior high schools report a high degree of discipline problems, it may be due to excessive control over students at a period in their lives when they need more autonomy (Eccles et al., 1991). They conducted a longitudinal study of 2,300 sixth- and seventh-grade students to test the hypothesis. The researchers found that both students and teachers reported that students had fewer decision-making opportunities in junior high school than they did in elementary school. The students who reported the least amount of involvement with classroom decision making were the students who physically matured the earliest. The researchers were not sure whether this was because the teachers treated them differently or because the students perceived the environment differently, but one thing was certain: by the end of the school year, the most mature students reported twice as often as the less-mature students that they didn't have a say, but should have one, in decisions about what they would learn, how they would learn it, or what the classroom rules would be.

Students who perceived the most constraints on their autonomy were the ones who showed the greatest decline in intrinsic motivation toward school and, consequently, the greatest amount of misbehavior. The researchers concluded that the environment was mismatched to the students' developmental levels. "When they move into junior high school, many early adolescents experience a decrease in the opportunity to participate in classroom decision-making, and this decrease is accompanied by a decrease in intrinsic motivation and an increase in school misbehavior" (Eccles et al., 1991, p. 66). Maslow might conclude that these students were being frustrated in their attempts to become self-actualized. In any case, schools should attempt to be flexible enough to find a level of control that fosters positive growth without undermining intrinsic motivation to learn, and the level of control must decrease as children become older and have more desire for autonomy. The idea of giving students reasonable options in deciding what they will study and how they will learn coincides with Wlodkowski's (1986) suggestions for techniques that help students fulfill their need for self-actualization.

Students sometimes misbehave in order to feel more in control of their particular situations. In one study, researchers polled 127 students, 54 with learning disabilities and 73 in regular education, to determine, among other things, how their perceived control correlated with their level of misbehavior (Heavey et al., 1989). Overall, the students who reported the highest degree of perceived self-control over the school environment were found to exhibit more misbehavior than students who felt they were less in control of their lives in school. This finding seems to contradict the assumption that students who feel least in control will have the most behavior problems, but the researchers postulated that the reason the high-control students felt in control in the first place was because they were wielding some power over their environment by misbehaving.

Whereas perceived control describes an individual's perceptions about a certain situation, another term, *locus of control,* describes a person's general outlook and is an additional factor in behavior and motivation. People with an internal locus of control believe they are responsible for their actions; those with an external locus believe forces beyond their control are running their lives. One study indicated that certain students who have an internal locus are better able to improve their behavioral motivation than are other students with an external locus (Swenson & Kennedy, 1995). The researchers examined the results of intervention strategies used with 307 teenage males who were classified as juvenile offenders. The study found that many students responded better to behavioral interventions when they attributed success to their own behavior and when they were concerned about their delinquent activities, instead of thinking nothing was wrong. The researchers suggested that to change the negative behaviors of these students, treatment should emphasize the individual's control over his own environment. They urged that the students should not be blamed for their current situations, but at the same time should be made aware that they were responsible for changing their situations.

ASSESSING STUDENT MOTIVATION

It is helpful for a teacher to assess the degree of a student's motivation to behave and to learn. Once this has been accomplished, the teacher can probe for underlying factors that are negatively influencing the motivation, and can subsequently design instructional or environmental modifications. Assessment of motivation can be as simple as observing a student and noting that the student pays no attention to lessons, but instead talks to friends constantly. Or, the teacher can make the assessment a bit more controlled and ask the student questions or have the student complete a survey. For example, researchers in Wisconsin conducted an experiment in which elementary students filled out a survey about their behaviors, identified areas they would like to improve, and then met with teachers on a regular basis to discuss their progress (Klausmeier & Ghatala, 1971). Students rated themselves on twenty academic and behavioral factors such as "I listen to the teacher," "I do extra schoolwork," and "I help my classmates." The teachers also rated the students. Using the assessment information, the teachers worked with the students to improve the targeted behaviors, holding conferences with students at regular intervals to discuss progress. The researchers recorded a great deal of enthusiasm among students for the project, and by the end of the school year, students' and teachers' ratings of student behavior had increased across the board. In contrast to exhibiting the usual misbehavior at the end of the year, students who participated in the project "kept up their academic work right to the last day of school, and discipline was no problem" (p. 348). This appears to be another example of how student motivation to engage in appropriate behaviors can increase when students feel they have some control in the decisions about their lives.

It is easy to see how an individual classroom teacher might adapt the techniques of this study to fit her needs. Having students answer questions about their motivation and their perceptions of their behavior would be a valuable first step in creating individualized goals for those students whose behavior is less than acceptable. This particular study did not ask students questions about their perceived degree of control in the classroom, but a few simple questions of that type would help a teacher determine whether some students might be misbehaving because they feel they have no control. The teacher could then make some changes in the classroom environment, giving students more choices and options.

MOTIVATION AND MISBEHAVIOR

Motivation is sometimes thought of as the feelings students get in accepting a challenge or in demonstrating a competence, even if the challenge is to do something wrong. "Some misbehavior reflects proactive efforts to do things that will lead to such feelings; other behavior reflects reactive efforts to deal with threats that interfere with such feelings" (Adelman & Taylor, 1990, p. 543). For example, a student who sets off the fire alarm is taking a proactive step, seeking the challenge of breaking the law and looking for the feeling of competence that will result if he does not get caught. To prevent misbehavior, Adelman and Taylor recommended that teachers and administrators change the student's environment so that it is more intrinsically motivating. Misbehaving often produces more intrinsic rewards than does participating in school, the writers acknowledged, and therefore, to prevent misbehavior in students who are so inclined, "alternatives must be capable of producing greater feelings of self-determination, competence, and relatedness that usually result from the youngster's deviant actions" (p. 346). Unfortunately for the classroom teacher, this can be difficult; the writers recognized this, and concluded that the teacher sometimes must find alternatives "well beyond the norm" (p. 347) of what would typically be offered in the classroom. In addition, Adelman & Taylor (1990) suggest teachers must be willing to put up with a continuation of some otherwise unacceptable behavior until the intrinsic rewards of the new activities extinguish the misbehavior.

Example

A daily report card system worked for an eighth-grade student, "Tim," who exhibited inappropriate classroom behavior and was failing four of his six classes (Fairchild, 1983). The parents wanted a system that would revoke privileges when Tim behaved inappropriately or did not make an effort at school. The school developed a daily report card in which each of Tim's teachers would rate his behavior and effort as excellent, good, OK, or poor. If he received negative comments, Tim would have to come home immediately after school and could not watch television, listen to the stereo, or use the phone. Tim was told he could terminate the daily report card system when he had ten consecutive school days with no negative comments. After 75 days, Tim achieved his goal. Before and after the intervention, teachers rated Tim on a scale of 1 (unacceptable) to 4 (excellent) in behavior and effort. Before the program, he received average ratings of 1.4 in behavior and 1.8 in effort; three weeks after the report card system ended, he received ratings of 3.8 in behavior and 4.0 in effort. His grade-point average rose from 1.71 soon after the program began to 2.86 at the end of the school year. And perhaps most indicative of his increased motivation to learn and behave, Tim requested to return to the daily report card system for a short period when his grades began to slip again.

CONCLUSION

When teachers consider that misbehavior can be viewed as a manifestation of some unfulfilled need, they can look for ways to satisfy that need. Said another way, the teacher can look for aspects of the child's environment that are missing or inadequately provided. The process is not as complicated as it sounds; oftentimes all it takes is for the teacher to talk to the student. The teacher may have to make a few accommodations and adaptions to create a more motivating environment for the student, but the teacher will soon discover that a student whose basic needs are fulfilled and who is given room to pursue his growth needs is a well-behaved student. The additional, individualized adaptations will have been worth the effort.

REFERENCES

Adelman, H. S., and Taylor, L.: Intrinsic motivation and school misbehavior: Some intervention implications. *Journal Of Learning Disabilities, 23*(9), 541–550, 1990.

Carnes, A. W., and Carns, M. R.: Making behavioral contracts successful. *School Counselor, 42*(2), 155–160, 1994.

Eccles, J. S., Buchanan, C. M., Flanagan, C., Fuligni, A., Midgeley, C., and Yee, D.: Control verses autonomy during early adolescence. *Journal of Social Issues, 47*(4), 53–68, 1991.

Fairchild, T. F.: Effects of a daily report card system on an eighth grader exhibiting behavioral and motivational problems. *School Counselor, 31*(1), 83–86, 1983.

Gerardi, M. B.: Discipline is no problem with my middle school Student of the Week. *Clearing House, 54*, (8), 381, 1981.

Heavey, C. L., Adelman, H. S., Nelson, P., and Smith, D. C.: Learning problems, anger, perceived control, and misbehavior. *Journal of Learning Disabilities, 22*(1), 46–50, 1989.

Klausmeier, H. J., and Ghatala, E.: Individually guided motivation: Developing self direction and prosocial behaviors. *Elementary School Journal, 71*(6), 339–350, 1971.

McDaniel, T. R.: Identifying discipline problems. *Childhood Education,* March/April, 223–225, 1981.

Maslow, A. H.: *Motivation and Personality.* New York: Harper Collins, 15–26, 1970.

Swenson, C. C., and Kennedy, W.: Perceived control and treatment outcome with chronic adolescent offenders. *Adolescence, 30*(119), 565–577, 1995.

Wlodkowski, R. J.: *Motivation and Teaching: A Practical Guide.* Washington, National Education Association, 59–81, 1986.

Chapter 4

PREVENTION OF PROBLEMS

It is safe to say that it is easier and more desirable to prevent discipline problems than it is to deal with them when they occur. If teachers are not especially careful, it is possible for disruptive and unacceptable student behavior to slowly but steadily appear in the classroom. "Over time, almost imperceptibly, expectations of what constitutes acceptable behavior get redefined. We gradually tolerate more and more, until what once was unthinkable becomes the new norm" (American Federation of Teachers, 1995-96, p. 24).

In planning to prevent discipline problems before they occur, it is important for teachers to reflect on some possible reasons why a student misbehaves or breaks the established rules. Albert (1995) claims that some students are trying to get extra attention while others are trying to be "the boss." Some students, she opines, are trying to get even for a real or imagined injustice, and others are compensating for their feelings of inadequacy or lack of confidence. Without question there are a host of reasons why students disrupt the orderly process of the class. Some of those reasons can be identified but many cannot. The important thing to do is to try to prevent discipline problems before they occur, and there are many important steps teachers can take to prevent discipline problems from developing. McCormack (1989) identifies four qualities of effective schools that can be applied to preventing discipline problems: (1) Teachers should have high expectations of students, and they should communicate those expectations regularly. (2) Teachers should monitor student behavior consistently (3) Teachers must share the responsibility for discipline with principals and assistant principals, and finally, (4) teachers should foster home/school relations by keeping the parents informed and involved.

There is considerable evidence to show that students sincerely want discipline and order in their classes. Winik (1996) reports on a focus group of urban and suburban high school students who discussed the schools they attended and the educations they were receiving. "According to these students, what their schools most lack—and what students most want—are discipline and order" (p. 12). When they were asked to grade the personal behavior at their school, most of the group gave their peers and, importantly, their teachers only Cs and Ds. They point out that many teachers fail to exert their authority in the classrooms. If teachers don't establish control, one student observed, some of their students will walk all over them. "The relationship between discipline and education is complex. On the one hand, some teacher authority in the service of classroom order is essential to education. The alternative is a mild Hobbesian state of war, where competition for attention, status, power, and survival take precedence over academic learning" (Kann, 1994, p. 71).

Discipline problems can usually be prevented by establishing and maintaining an effective and efficient system of classroom management. "A teacher who has mastered classroom management skills keeps students constructively engaged and learning from the moment they enter the room until the time they leave" (American Federation of Teachers, 1995-96 p. 24). It is important from the very beginning to establish that classroom management and discipline are not the same thing. Discipline is a major part of classroom management, and it is reactive in nature. Teachers react or respond to student behavior that disrupts the good order of the classroom. Classroom management can be seen as proactive. It is preventative, and its goal is self-control on the part of the students. The issue in any system of classroom management is whether the students are under self-control or teacher control. Ideally, the self-control inherent in a good system of classroom management is preferred.

According to Eggen and Kauchak (1997) the two major goals of classroom management are:

1. Create the best learning environment possible.
2. Develop student responsibility and self-regulation.

Classroom management means establishing and maintaining a routine in the classroom that allows teaching and learning to proceed effectively.

A complete system of classroom management consists of many components, the first of which is *planning*.

PLANNING

A shrewd teacher will invest a considerable amount of time in planning the implementation of a system of classroom management. Canter (1996) establishes a new set of basics in preparing for the possibility of discipline problems. He indicates that it is important to model trust and respect for the students. He urges teachers to get to know their students as individuals and to establish strong ties with the home. He points out that students need structure and identifies behavior limits and that they should be directly taught the behaviors which are expected of them. In other words teachers should have and follow a discipline plan. But he cautions, "To be successful, a discipline plan should be built on a foundation of mutual trust and respect" (Canter, 1996, p. 12).

Planning a system of classroom management requires both reflection and anticipation. It is important to reflect on previous experiences and to think about the possible problems that could occur if teachers haven't prepared for them. "A good classroom manager carefully plans everything that occurs in the classroom from the seating arrangements to instructions for children who finish planned activities early" (American Federation of Teachers, 1995-96, p. 24). In thinking about establishing a system of classroom management and realizing that positive, well managed classrooms do not happen automatically, a number of important questions come to mind.

1. How can I legitimately make students feel good about themselves and want to participate?
2. How much control of the classroom do I want to exercise?
3. How do I develop healthy, appropriate relationships with students?
4. What are the different ways I can use to communicate with students?
5. What do I have to do to keep the students engaged?
6. What rules should I have in my classroom?
7. Should I employ particular seating arrangements?
8. What issues should I consider in grouping students for academic work and social activities?
9. What should I require or allow when students finish their work before the other students?
10. How should I prepare for the many transitions that occur each day?

Thinking about questions like these and many others that any teacher can easily think of dramatizes the importance of careful planning. Without a carefully constructed classroom management plan, teachers may develop defensive reactions to disruptive students and this will most certainly seriously compromise their effectiveness as teachers.

FACTORS OF PLANNING TO CONSIDER

Planning for classroom management requires a teacher to consider at least two major factors. The first factor is the types of students who will be in the class. Are they primary, intermediate, middle school, or high school? What are their ages? Younger children tend to be more compliant while older children tend to respond more to reason and rationales. Middle school children often want to test the limits and exert their independence. Another issue regarding the type of student is potential or ability level. More able students work well without constant supervision, while less able students often need to be reminded of the rules and their responsibilities.

The second factor to consider is the ecology of the classroom. Are the children situated so they can see the chalkboard and hear the teacher? Are they sitting by an antagonist or a friend who may coerce them into misbehavior? Are the traffic patterns such that students have unfettered access to workstations, the teacher's desk, and the pencil sharpener?

Two of the most important aspects of a system of classroom management that require planning are the classroom rules and the procedures that will be employed in the classroom. Consideration of the type of children the teacher will have and the total ecology of the classroom are necessary in order to develop appropriate rules and procedures.

Rules

Rules can be considered the standards of acceptable behavior in the classroom. The students should be helped to see that the rules are necessary and fair. As a matter of fact, they should be allowed and encouraged to participate in the development of the classroom rules. Rich (1984) suggests that students will likely make a serious attempt to comply with rules they have had a hand in developing; consequently, they should help formulate the rules "to the extent that their understanding and responsibility will promote rather than detract from a sound learning environment" (p. 111). A wise teacher will gather the students together on the first day of school for discussion and development of the list of rules that will be used in the classroom. Similarly, she will frequently review the rules with the students, making sure they fully understand them.

It is not enough to simply create a complete set of rules or to have contingencies specified for the rules. Continual review of the rules and the consequences of violating them must occur. "In order to facilitate maximum compliance to classroom rules and expectations, . . . the contingencies or rules . . . must be well-articulated and reviewed prior to the start of the planned instructional activities" (Rosenberg, 1986, p. 246).

The manner in which classroom rules are enforced is open to continual scrutiny; therefore, "it is important that certain conditions be observed in handling rules if they are to be fair and effective" (Rich, 1984, p. 111). *Consistency* is perhaps the most important factor in enforcing classroom rules. A violation of the rule in one case must be a violation of the rule in another case. Similarly all students, both the academically strong and the academically weak, must be treated in exactly the same manner. It would be a disaster if a teacher were seen by her students as being unfair or as showing partiality to some students over others.

The classroom rules should be *consistent* with the school rules and the students should have that consistency emphasized and elaborated for them. The students should be provided rationales for the rules and enough time should be allocated for discussion of the rationales to assure that the students fully understand the reasons behind the rules.

The rules should be stated *positively* and not as a list of "do nots." Students should be helped to understand that the rules are expectations of positive behavior and not prohibitions of negative behavior. Classroom discussions about the expectation of appropriate behavior are an excellent way of facilitating student participation in the process.

The rules should be clear and precise, stated in a manner to minimize confusion or misunderstanding. Perhaps most importantly, the list of rules should be *short*. Don't clutter the process with a list of rules so long that the students will not be able to remember them. A short list, stated as positive expectations will provide the students with expectations of behavior that will be easy to understand and remember.

Procedures

Classroom procedures are the routines students will follow in executing the full complement of their responsibilities. There are a variety of situations for which established procedures are not only helpful but also necessary. Situations in the classroom requiring carefully developed procedures include:

- Student arrival and acceptable activities while waiting for the teacher to begin.
- What students may do when they have completed their seatwork.
- How homework and classwork are to be turned in.
- How to line up and execute a fire drill.
- How to ask for help from the teacher.
- What to do in transitions such as
    - Going to lunch.
    - Returning from recess.
    - Cleaning up at the end of the day.

Teachers who anticipate situations that will require procedures and develop procedures in advance for them, will have those situations unfold in an orderly and nondisruptive manner. Not anticipating the procedures that will be required in certain situations will inevitably lead to chaos. When procedures have been established, it is imperative to review and rehearse them until they become automatic. Teachers should strive to have students *overlearn* the classroom procedures that will be employed that year.

After the rules have been developed and the procedures have been established, planning a variety of instructional variables is necessary.

Teaching and Instruction

The process of instruction or the teaching activities designed to facilitate student learning, provides ample opportunity for planning to prevent discipline problems. For example, the myriad of logistical factors a teacher must confront require considerable forethought and planning. In most classrooms for at least a portion of the day, the teacher is involved with a small group while the rest of the students are engaged in seatwork. Consideration must be given to how the teacher will work successfully with the group and at the same time monitor the behavior of the rest of the class. The teacher must position herself so as to be able to work efficiently with her group and also watch the students doing seatwork. She should also look up frequently and catch the eye of any student in her seat who is looking up from her work. The impression will be that the teacher is always watching.

Another instructional issue to be anticipated is the manner in which the teacher wants the students to verbalize in class. Are they expected to raise their hands at all times and wait to be acknowledged before speaking? Are there certain situations where spontaneous verbalizing may be accepted or even encouraged? Clearly the more such factors are anticipated and planned, the more smoothly the process will go.

Self-directed seatwork poses unique problems that call for careful planning. Are the students allowed to quietly talk occasionally, or are they expected to remain totally silent? What are they expected or allowed to do when they finish their work? Do they bring their completed work to the teacher, or do they keep it to be collected? The more students understand the expectations teachers have, the more likely they are to comply and not create disruptions.

Logistics

The issue of the bell ringing to signal a change of classes or the end of the day suggests the need for special planning. What does the bell mean to the teacher? Does she consider it a signal to her or a signal to the students? Anticipating an issue like this and communicating expectations to students will prevent disruptions of order and possible discipline problems. For example, a teacher might explain to her students that the bell is a signal to her and not to the students. She would make it clear that students are not to put their supplies away and leave their seats until she gives them permission to do so. The importance of such an established procedure is made abundantly clear the first time a teacher tries to finish a point or draw a close to a lesson with students putting away their books and leaving their seats.

Another logistical issue is the decision to use special signals which call for a certain type of behavior. Some teachers turn the classroom lights on and off when they want the students to observe absolute silence. Other teachers raise their hand and hold it aloft until all the students stop what they are doing and attend fully to the teacher. If signals are employed, it is imperative that the students fully understand the behavior that is expected of them.

There are also several issues of classroom geography that require consideration. Perhaps one of the first issues to be planned is the seating arrangements for the students. Will the teacher use rows of seats, semi-circular seating, or clusters of seats. Will she assign students to their seats or allow them to sit wherever they choose on any given day? Clearly there are consequences to any of the possible answers to these questions, but more importantly there are consequences to not planning for these questions. For example, not planning for seating arrangements could have a deleterious effect on student participation in instructional activities. If a teacher is attempting to have a debate and she has the students sitting in rows, it may well be less satisfactory than if they were sitting in a circle. More importantly chaos could reign with students moving about, talking only to the teacher, or initiating private conversations. In such unplanned situations, discipline problems are inevitable.

In order to prevent discipline problems, another major issue requiring planning is the traffic flow of the classroom. Think of the possible disruptions that could occur if students have to cut between desks or through groups to hand in work or to come to the teacher's desk. The students should be fully aware of the teacher's expectations regarding acceptable traffic patterns to her desk, the pencil sharpener, or a particular learning center.

A final point among the many that require planning is the issue of teacher mobility. Is the room set up in such a way as to allow the teacher to move freely about the room without disturbing students who are working? The more students are disrupted the more likely is the chance that there will be discipline problems.

Teacher Characteristics

The most important instructional variable is the teacher. The characteristics of the teacher are important and reflection upon them virtually requires her to plan appropriately to minimize the chances of discipline problems. For example, where does the teacher stand on the issue of firmness in terms of dealing with students? All teachers fall somewhere on the continuum of autocratic to democratic, and a teacher's position on that continuum creates certain consequences in the classroom. For example, a teacher who attempts to be too autocratic may be causing student to confrontations, them while being too democratic may invite anarchy.

How teachers respond to students is an issue all teachers must confront. Who doesn't want to be liked? The mistake many teachers, especially new teachers, make is trying to be liked before they are respected. If a teacher first gains the students, respect, they also in time will be liked by them. There is a great deal of truth in the old bromide that a teacher "can be *friendly* with students but cannot be *friends* with them".

Eggen and Kauchak (1997) suggest three important teacher skills are exceedingly helpful in preventing discipline problems. These skills are organization, lesson flow, and communication.

Organization

In terms of organization, it is imperative for teachers to be prepared to teach. To be unprepared is an invitation for disorder and disruption. Teachers must have their lessons carefully planned and their teaching materials prepared and ready to use. To be unsure about what to do next or to discover that you do not have your worksheets ready to pass out is to create an opportunity for disruptions or discipline problems to occur. Students who are kept involved in the teaching/learning activity do not have the opportunity to disrupt their neighbor, laugh at an antic, or begin whispering to a friend. It is often the case that legitimate discipline problems occur when teachers have to confront such minor transgressions.

Another organizational skill that will help prevent discipline problems is the effective use of time. Teachers are wise to begin the day and all lessons on time. It is also advantageous to keep the students engaged for the duration of the activity. Students who are waiting for the teacher or have nothing to do are more likely than engaged students to make mischief. Even relatively innocent mischief or "kibitzing around," when multiplied over several students or groups of students, creates a disturbance sufficient to disrupt the learning of the students in the class. It becomes almost inevitably a situation with which the teacher must deal.

Lesson Flow

Establishing effective and efficient routines is a skill that typically develops with experience, and it is invaluable in preventing disruptions or discipline problems. Handing in homework, completing in-class assignments, taking a test, going to music, and being dismissed are all activities made more efficient by having established and rehearsed in advance the routines students are to follow.

The skill and efficiency with which the teacher keeps the lesson moving is another important consideration in preventing disturbances or disruptions. The ability to prevent dead time and the time students are off task will also prove to be an effective deterrent of discipline problems. Similarly, a teacher's ability to know what is going on everywhere in the classroom, even while she is occupied, is something that is exceedingly helpful in nipping potential problems in the bud. Kounin (1970) coined the now-famous term "withitness" to describe knowing what's going on all the time and conveying to the students that she knows what is going on. Withitness is clearly a characteristic that helps immeasurably in preventing discipline problems.

Communication

Among the many teacher skills that can help in the prevention of discipline problems, a final consideration will be given to the manner in which a teacher expresses herself to her students. Experienced teachers know that tone of voice, body posture, and facial expression are powerful tools of communication that teachers can use strategically to prevent problems before they blow up.

Preventing discipline problems makes life in the classroom considerably more comfortable for the teacher than having to deal with them when they occur. Planning is the key to prevention and among the many areas requiring careful teacher planning, several have been touched on here. The most important factor in preventing discipline problems is arguably the *persona of the teacher*. Those teachers who earn their students' respect will unquestionably encounter favor and less severe discipline problems than those who are not respected as highly. The first and best strategy of earning student respect is to respect them. If teachers treat students fairly and courteously, they are well on their way to earning student respect. The other essential aspect of a teacher's persona that significantly contributes to the prevention of discipline problems is the teacher's consistency. If teachers are consistent in the way they execute the classroom procedures and enforce the classroom rules, the likelihood of the prevention of discipline problems will increase. Similarly, the consistency manifested in treating all children exactly the same cannot be overemphasized. These aspects of the teacher's persona, coupled with Kounin's concept of withitness (or complete awareness of what's going on in the classroom), will significantly help in the prevention of discipline problems.

REFERENCES

Albert, L.: Discipline: Is it a dirty word? *Learning,* September, 43–46, 1995.

American Federation of Teachers: Elements of an effective discipline strategy. *American Educator, 19*(4), 24–27, 1995-96.

Canter, L.: First, the rapport–then, the rules. *Learning,* March/April, 12–14, 1996.

Eggen, P., and Kauchak, D.: *Educational Psychology Windows on Classrooms.* Upper Saddle River, N.J., Prentice Hall, 1997.

Kann, M. E.: Discipline, character, and education. *Teaching Education, 6* (1), 71–75, 1994.

Kounin, J.: *Discipline and Group Management in the Classroom.* New York, Holt Rinehart, 1970.

McCormack, S.: Prevention–not punishment–is the key to effective discipline. *Executive Educator, 11*(1), 25–26, 1989.

Rich, J.M.: Discipline, rules, and punishment. *Contemporary Education, 55*(2), 110-112, 1984.

Rosenberg, M. S.: Maximizing the effectiveness of structured classroom management programs: Implementing rule-review procedures with disruptive and distractible students. *Behavioral Disorders, 11*, 239–249, 1986.

Winik, L. W.: Students want more discipline, disruptive classmates out. *American Educator*, Fall, 12–14, 1996.

Chapter 5

DEALING WITH PROBLEMS

The question of what is a discipline problem, is not as simple as it may appear. "To teachers, however, discipline should suggest a range of practices that contribute to a well-managed classroom in which students enjoy going about the business of learning" (Smith & Misra, 1992, p. 353). No student is perfectly behaved all the time, and student "imperfections" may range from simple inattention to engaging in a fistfight in class. It is helpful to think of such situations as a continuum from not really being a problem to constituting a major problem with which the teacher needs assistance. Something that may be annoying but not really a problem could be a student's mind wandering or not following directions. Examples of minor problems might be seat leaving, passing notes, or disturbing a neighbor. Major problems would certainly include open defiance, violence, or possession of drugs. Of course, there could be an infinite number of gradations of severity along the continuum, and the teacher must make the ultimate call as to whether something is or is not a discipline problem.

In Chapter 4 the importance of the teacher's personality in preventing discipline problems was highlighted. The same is equally true when it comes to dealing with discipline problems. All teachers at one time or another must deal with discipline problems in the classroom, in the hallways, or on the school grounds. It is a fact that teachers who are respected by students encounter fewer discipline problems over the course of a week, a year, or a career than teachers who are not respected by their students.

The problem for some teachers is associated with their attitude about student respect. Some teachers feel it is their inalienable right as a teacher to receive unqualified student respect. Unfortunately, as much as we want to believe that all students should naturally respect all teachers, it simply doesn't happen that way. In reality every teacher must *earn* the respect of students. Earning respect requires conscious effort; it doesn't just happen.

The first step in earning and maintaining student respect is to overtly respect the students. Teachers should model respect for the students by virtue of the way they interact with them. Teachers can show respect for students by
- being polite and courteous,
- never humiliating or embarrassing them,
- being encouraging and expressing confidence in them,
- assuring that others in the class show respect, and
- dealing with their indiscretions privately whenever possible.

Far too many new teachers are overly and unnecessarily concerned about being liked by the students. To some degree this is an understandable concern and one that is also shared to some degree by all teachers. It is imperative for teachers, especially new teachers, to understand (and embrace) that respect is the essential prerequisite to being liked. Teachers must consciously address the issue of earning student respect. If that objective is successfully accomplished, the issue of being liked by the students will take care of itself.

Teachers are often reminded about how important it is to develop rapport with their students. Rapport can be thought of as the ability to interact effectively both in formal instruction and in informal interaction with students. Rapport does not necessarily mean being liked or being popular. It is predicated on respect, and it is an invaluable asset in dealing with the variety of disruptions and discipline problems teachers inevitably encounter.

Another aspect of the teacher's personality worth mentioning is the perception that they are fair. Students readily accept and, in fact, want teachers who maintain order and discipline in the classroom. They only ask that teachers maintain fairness. In other words, they want teachers to consistently interpret and enforce the rules and treat all students the same. "Failing to impose a discipline plan consistently breeds divisiveness and contempt–regardless of how right you believe it is to make an exception 'just this once' " (Lawrence & Olvey, 1994, p. 31).

TYPES OF PROBLEMS

The types of problems teachers have to confront are extremely varied and range from very minor infractions to disruptions of a most serious nature. Of the myriad of problems, the ones that teachers are most concerned about (Friedberg et al., 1995; Rogers, 1995; Lawrence & Kant, 1994; Reissman, 1993; Alley et al., 1990) include:

- violence
- drugs and alcohol
- intruding
- fighting
- false fire alarms
- defiance and non-compliance
- vandalism
- insubordination
- argumentativeness
- stealing

There are also a host of less serious but more frequent student behaviors that teachers must deal with such as sulking, interrupting, seat leaving, talking out, and teasing. A measure of the seriousness of an event can be the degree to which it jeopardizes the safety of other students and teachers, and the degree to which it disrupts the orderly functioning of the classroom. The teacher's response must always take into consideration safety first and then the issue of order and effective functioning.

RESPONDING TO PROBLEMS

The manner in which teachers respond to discipline problems depends on the type of problem exhibited. It would not be appropriate to react to an episode of inattention in the same way required by an act of violence. Various types of teacher reactions to a variety of discipline problems are depicted below in a discipline staircase (Figure 5.1).

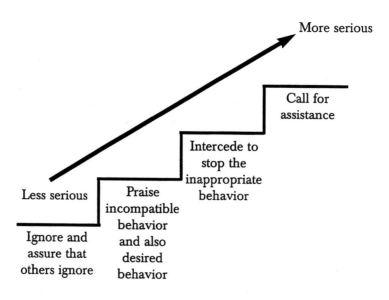

Figure 5.1. Discipline Staircase

As important as it is for teachers to respond appropriately to discipline problems, it is equally important not to overreact in such situations. Care must be exercised by teachers not to browbeat and berate students unnecessarily; they typically do not want to intimidate their students, and they want to be careful not to exclusively rely on power when relating to students. "When teachers misuse authority, they tend to reinforce youngsters' sense of weakness, passivity, subordination, and victimization. Often students react to this pattern of discipline in self destructive or educationally dysfunctional ways" (Kann, 1994, p. 72).

SPECIFIC STRATEGIES

Keeping in mind the discipline staircase depicted in Figure 5.1, it is appropriate to consider strategies that range from those used for minor infractions to those needed for more serious problems. Experience in the classroom and a teacher's good judgment help considerably in determining which strategy to employ in a given situation.

Ignore the Inappropriate Behavior

Without a doubt, the most difficult skill for a teacher to master is the skill of ignoring inappropriate student behavior. It is almost an instinctive reaction to respond to a misbehaving student. At one time or another, we have all been guilty of letting "the squeaky wheel get the grease." It takes a conscious act and lots of practice to consistently ignore a student who is acting out. It is even a bit more complicated when teachers realize that they must also assure that others ignore the behaviors too.

To understand the importance of ignoring untoward behavior, it is necessary to review the effects of positive reinforcement and extinction. Whenever a teacher attends to inappropriate behavior, he is positively reinforcing that behavior. Even a rebuke serves as positive reinforcement because it is teacher attention. Positive reinforcement causes a behavior to increase, and this explains why some children continue to misbehave, even after they have been "reminded" or scolded. On the other hand, if no attention (teacher or peer) is forthcoming, the behavior is not reinforced and, in time, extinction will occur. In other words, the undesirable behavior will cease.

Once again the importance of consistency is made clear. Consistently ignoring the behavior results in success; inconsistency results in strengthening the undesirable behavior. One way for a teacher to improve his ability to ignore inappropriate behavior is to consistently reinforce other students who are engaging in appropriate behavior. For example, if Cathy is attempting to chat with a neighbor, don't correct her. Rather, praise Kristen who is working quietly and remaining on task and ignore Cathy's inappropriate behavior. Naturally, praise and compliment Cathy as soon as she returns to task. "Students notice what the teacher does attend to—students who follow the rule and put their hand up and wait—and they often follow suit" (Rogers, 1995, p. 18). If John is leaving his seat regularly, ignore it, but praise him when he is in his seat. This is referred to as reinforcing an incompatible behavior (sitting is incompatible with seat leaving), and is a very effective way of creating appropriate behavior and ignoring inappropriate behavior. Of utmost importance, *be consistent!*

The "I Mean Business" Look

Another strategy to employ with student behaviors that are annoying but not harmful is the *"I mean business"* stare. This is a strategy that requires no talking on the part of the teacher, but one that is very effective if employed promptly. Children have often reported that they always know their parent(s) meant business by that "look" in their eye. The same phenomena occurs between students and teachers. If Gracelyn is putting on lipstick instead of attending to the problem at the chalkboard, the teacher can almost always get her immediately back on task by giving her that *"you'd better get to work, young lady"* stare. Gracelyn's knowing the teacher saw her and disapproved of what she was doing, is usually all that is required to get her to refocus. Developing that special glance or look is a skill all teachers can easily master with just a little practice. It is a strategy that doesn't call attention to a student and avoids the possibility of public humiliation. "A student who's openly chastised, ostracized, or punished won't readily become a classroom contributor" (Reissman, 1993, p. 48).

Move to the Problem

A teacher's movement about the room is obviously important for instructional reasons, and it is also a very important strategy to employ in dealing with many discipline problems. Moving to an area proximate to the child or children causing the disruption most often causes the misbehavior to desist and the children to return to task. It signals to them that the teacher is not only acutely aware of their misbehavior, but that he is poised and ready to deal with it. If Pam and Jenny are exchanging notes and whispering instead of paying attention and participating in the learning activity, a shrewd teacher will simply move to a location between or very near their desks. It won't be necessary for him to say a word to them; he will just continue to teach from that location. The girls will not be able to continue their disruptive activity. Reissman (1993) points out that this strategy would produce two significant advantages. First, instruction would not have been interrupted and the disruption would have been stopped. Second, Pam and Jenny were not embarrassed by a public chastisement, and they can easily rejoin the activity.

Having students expect you to be moving about the classroom and your moving quickly to potential trouble spots will serve as a highly effective strategy of dealing with disruptions and potential disruptions.

Dramatic Pause and Change in Voice

Rogers (1995) suggests that a thoughtful use of a dramatic pause can be an effective tool. If a teacher is explaining something and Marianne is whispering to Eleanor, the teacher might abruptly stop talking in mid-sentence, stare at Marianne, and then in a lower, more serious tone say, "Everyone needs to pay careful attention to what I'm saying." Then he would immediately go on with his explanation without specifically targeting Marianne with a reprimand.

Deal with It Immediately

When there is a problem of any kind, it is imperative not to put it off and attempt to deal with it later. In the same way that trying to positively reinforce a good behavior two hours later doesn't work, it is also ineffective to deal with a discipline problem at the end of the period or later in the day. In virtually every situation, it is better to employ a discipline strategy at the moment the infraction occurs. For example, if a teacher sees George copying answers from Emma's test paper, he should deal with George at that moment. He could walk to George's desk and simply take away his test paper, or he could quietly tell George that if his eyes wander again, he will receive a zero on the test.

Don't Debate

The possibility exists, especially with older students, that in a situation similar to the one described above, a student could become argumentative, claiming that she wasn't cheating. The important rule of thumb in such situations is to never debate the student, either publically or privately about the issue. Some students will try to engage the teacher in a power struggle by attempting to argue the point. In such situations, Rogers (1995) suggests that teachers, "remain assertive but civil, redirect the student to the primary issue . . . and don't capitulate to secondary behavior by discussion, argument, or adversarial tactics" (p. 19).

For example, a student who has just been dealt with for annoying a neighbor may become argumentative and claim that she wasn't bothering the neighbor, but rather just asking her what the assignment was. Care must be exercised not to get trapped into debating whether or not she was bothering her neighbor, or whether or not it is permissible to ask a neighbor what the assignment is. Don't debate anything; just deal with the primary issue and simply move on.

Generating Interest

It is often a fact that students who disrupt or cause trouble are the students who are disinterested in the lesson or generally bored with school. Rather than deal with their disruptions, teachers would be better served if they attempted to co-opt them into participating and setting a good example for their students. A way to accomplish this seemingly difficult task is to use the student's interest in the particular activity. In other words, attempt to integrate the interests of potential troublemakers into the regular classroom activities. Suppose Linwood is an uncooperative, nonparticipator in math. The teacher is aware of his fanatical interest in cars. Perhaps the teacher could get Linwood involved by involving the class in math lessons that focus on the price, payment schedule, and upkeep expenses of different used cars. Similarly, the speed of different cars could be incorporated into a series of math problems.

As another example, suppose that Libby is a sulker who claims that she is always being picked on. Rather than complete her math assignments, which she could easily do, she sulks and withdraws from the interaction of the lesson. Perhaps the teacher ascertains that she, like many girls her age, is interested in makeup. A creative teacher could easily construct a variety of problems, activities, and lessons that focus on the purchase and use of makeup but that also teach the math skills the teacher has targeted.

Role playing, contests between teams of students, and the use of current events are but a few of the many additional strategies a teacher can employ to develop and maintain the interest of otherwise disinterested students. The goal is to find ways to ease them into the ongoing activities of the classroom.

Focus on What Students Value

Students come to school with some kind of value system intact. It frequently doesn't consist of the values teachers would like for students to embrace, but each and every student has learned to value certain things. Some students value being perceived as a rebel and non-conformist. Some students value authority while others place value on their perceived right to do or say whatever they want to whomever they want.

Sometimes the students' values can be used in dealing with inflammatory or potentially inflammatory situations. If a teacher observes Hannah glancing or staring at Franklin's seatwork, it may be possible to quickly terminate Hannah's undesirable behavior by quickly reminding her about trust and how important it is for a young girl to maintain the trust of her teachers and parents. If Miguel is fooling around with the classroom weather station, it may simply be enough to remind him how much it would cost to replace and that he and his family would be responsible if he broke it.

There are many things students value that can be used effectively by teachers to change student behavior. Trust, respect, courtesy, kindness, and authority are just a few.

It may be appropriate here to point out that there are times when a teacher simply cannot get to the bottom of a situation. Teachers should remember to try never to overreact in such a situation. For example, if no one will own up to drawing a funny picture on the chalkboard, it wouldn't be appropriate to ground the entire class from recess for a week. It is a good idea to recognize that there are some situations that will occur where the perpetrator(s) will not be identified for appropriate action. In such cases the teacher can choose one of several courses of action. Perhaps the teacher could approach the situation with humor. For example, on seeing a picture drawn on the chalkboard, the teacher might announce with a chuckle that the artist needs to pay more attention in art class. Another approach would be to simply erase the drawing without showing any emotion and go on with the lesson.

The Show Must Go On—Or Must It?

Occasionally circumstances emerge in the course of a day that make it very difficult for the teacher to control the group and begin the lesson. Students returning to class after a pep rally or exciting assembly is an example of such a situation. Teachers may fear that if they do not get the class under control and begin teaching, they will completely lose control entirely. Actually it might be better to "go along with the flow" for a few minutes and engage the class in a discussion about the upcoming baseball game or the presentation on drug abuse they just heard. The goal would be to involve as many students as possible in a general group discussion. This would eliminate private conversations and make it easier to draw closure and begin the planned lesson.

Remove Competing Objects

A source of disruption or a discipline problem is often objects students have found, been given, or brought to school that offer more attractiveness to the student than the teacher's lesson. These seductive objects include toys, candy, comic books, photographs, or notes. When a teacher observes that a student is attending to an object and not to the lesson, he should, without calling significant attention to the situation, simply remove the object from the student's possession. For example, during a social studies lesson, the teacher observes that Emma is reading a note. Not only is she distracted from the lesson, but she is also distracting Fanny and Catherine by showing them the note. Without stopping the lesson and without drawing attention, the teacher should walk to Emma's desk, reach down, confiscate the note, and move away from the area. If Emma attempts to put the note away as she sees the teacher approaching, he should put his hand out and quietly say "Give me the note". When she turns over the note, the teacher quietly says, "Thank you" and goes on with the lesson.

In the unlikely event that Emma would refuse to comply, more intrusive measures would be called for. These strategies will be addressed below.

Separate to Prevent Problems

One of the more intrusive strategies available to teachers is to separate a student from a situation or from other students. Often it is possible to avert a potentially explosive situation by employing this strategy. For example if a teacher notices that Jamal is trying to intimidate Mary into letting him copy from her paper, he could move Jamal's seat either temporarily or permanently. In some situations it may be more prudent and more effective to separate the one being "victimized" rather than the perpetrator. Suppose before class begins, Luther and his pals are trying to pick a fight with Roger. The teacher could unobtrusively intercede by asking Roger to perform an errand like erasing the chalkboard. Separating Roger from the situation avoids an explosive situation.

Reprimands

There are occasions, no matter how ingrained the importance of ignoring behavior is in a teacher's mind, when he must respond directly to a situation in the classroom. A student being careless with a pair of scissors or two students fighting on the floor are but two examples of situations that must be directly and immediately addressed. In such cases an immediate reprimand from the teacher is called for. The reprimand must be brief and delivered with a seriousness of tone that makes it clear that the teacher means business. The importance of keeping the reprimand brief cannot be overemphasized. The longer the reprimand, the longer the amount of time the teacher is attending to (and, in fact, reinforcing) the inappropriate behavior. In addition, the longer the reprimand, the greater the possibility and likelihood that the student will talk back. Of paramount importance is the teacher's recognition and understanding that he must not debate the student or discuss the situation in any way. If warranted, a discussion can take place after the situation has been resolved.

It is important for teachers to be specific when they choose to use a reprimand. Care must be exercised not to allow students who are behaving appropriately to infer that the reprimand is directed at them. It is essential for the teacher to direct the reprimand only at the student(s) who is acting out and to specify precisely what the student(s) is doing. For example, if Salvatore is teasing Carolyn by attempting to pull her chair out from under her, the teacher should immediately move to Salvatore's desk and emphatically say, "Stop moving her chair and get back to work right now!" The teacher should then turn away to indicate that there will be no discussion about the issue and give Salvatore a chance to comply. Kounin (1970) indicates that reprimands should be directed toward the targeted student and the targeted behavior. It should also identify an appropriate behavior that is incompatible with the misbehavior.

It is crucial for teachers to understand that the use of reprimands should be judiciously employed. One of the major mistakes inexperienced teachers make is to consistently use verbal reprimands when a student acts in any way inappropriately. This tends to create an extremely unsatisfactory scenario where the teacher is actually sustaining the inappropriate behavior by positively reinforcing the behavior through constant attention. The students learn, relatively early, that they can produce a predictable response from the teacher, and they tend to take advantage of this situation. A wise teacher will use reprimands judiciously and will make certain that the effect is an immediate change in student behavior.

Response-Cost

Punishment can often be a controversial topic in classrooms, primarily because it creates images of corporal punishment. The general concept of *punishment* should not be confused with spanking or whacks with a paddle. One form of punishment that teachers can use effectively and that does not require physical force is known as response-cost.

Basically, response-cost means that disruptive or otherwise inappropriate behavior will result in the loss of a predetermined amount of reinforcement. For example, seat leaving might result in the loss of ten minutes of free time or repeatedly disturbing a neighbor might result in the loss of the privilege of being a hall monitor. McClain and Kelley (1994) document the effectiveness of a response-cost program with three, eleven year old disruptive boys. They report dramatic improvement in the boys' behavior when compared to their baseline conditions and noticeably improved behavior when their behavior in the response-cost/school-home note condition is compared to their behavior in the school-home note without response-cost condition. "This type of intervention holds several advantages. First, this procedure can be easily implemented by general education classroom teachers without interfering with their lessons. Second, interventions such as this please parents of students with ADHD because many parents are concerned about general education teachers' ability to deal with their child's disorder . . ." (Bender &

Mathes, 1995, p. 230). We see response-cost operating in the natural environment all the time, and it is only natural to employ such strategies in the classroom. Parking tickets and cancellation of credit cards for failure to maintain payments are two examples of response-cost in the natural environment. A response-cost program is not unduly demanding in terms of teacher time. In fact, it has been demonstrated that in certain situations, students can manage the program themselves. "The student management and visual cuing of the free tokens minimize the demands on teacher time and offer elementary educators a practical and successful system for modifying behavior that is easy to implement within the constraints of the regular classroom setting. . . . the system is easily adaptable to a variety of behaviors that interfere with learning in the elementary classroom (e.g., calling out, out-of-seat, requests for teacher attention)" (Salend et al., 1988, p. 95).

Occasionally when response-cost is employed, teachers observe an increase in the frequency or intensity of the inappropriate behavior. This typically does not continue once the system of response-cost is in place. Teachers are encouraged to establish their systems to minimize such an increase when the reinforcer is removed. Smith and Misra (1992) suggest "minimizing the possibility of escalation by making the response-cost system part of a larger token economy where students also earn reinforcement for displaying appropriate behaviors" (p. 364).

Time-Out

Time-out is a procedure that is difficult to situate in the behavioral model. Some see it as an appropriate form of punishment because the aversive consequence of separation from the group has been added to the misbehaving student's environment. Others see it as a form of negative reinforcement because the aversive consequence of separation is removed and the student is allowed to return to the learning environment when she desists the inappropriate behavior during the time-out condition. Of course, the argument for extinction could also be made because in time out any inappropriate behavior is not reinforced and is allowed to extinguish.

However time-out is thought of, it is a popular strategy that teachers frequently use in discipline situations. Even though time-out is very popular, it is often misused and more often misunderstood. The misuse focuses on not fully understanding what time-out really means. It is important to understand that time-out is actually an abbreviation for "time out from positive reinforcement." Consequently, the effectiveness of time-out is severely limited if the learning environment is not systematically providing positive reinforcement for appropriate behavior, especially academic performance. During time-out access to positive reinforcement should be completely denied. Returning to the learning environment reestablishes the opportunity for the student to earn positive reinforcement.

Time-out can be implemented in a particular section of the classroom dedicated to that purpose, or in some cases, in another part of the school. Obviously a teacher should never use a dark, unventilated closet, a windowless area, or any other physically restrictive or uncomfortable space for the purpose of time-out. The purpose is to temporarily remove the disrupting child from the learning environment and from the schedule of positive reinforcement. Teachers must assure that other students do not provide attention or any kind of reinforcement to a child who has been placed in time-out. Time-out is an effective strategy but one which must be used with care. Smith and Misra (1992) caution that "teachers are strongly encouraged to make sure students are adequately monitored during time-out and that specific criteria guide reentry into the class" (p. 364).

If a separate room is used for time-out, the teacher or an aide should regularly monitor the student through a window.

Regular monitoring should also occur if the time-out area is a dedicated section of the classroom. No verbal exchange with the student should occur while she is in time-out, and no nonverbal interaction with other students should be allowed. The basic idea is that the separated student experience a period of isolation where she does not receive reinforcement of any kind. A teacher should have determined in advance the criteria that will be employed for reentry into the learning environment from the time-out area. In some cases a predetermined passage of time in the time-out condition could be used as the criterion. In other cases a behavioral criterion such as sitting quietly without disruption could be used as the criterion for reentry. As soon as a student returns to the learning environment, it is a good idea to find a legitimate reason to administer positive reinforcement to the student as quickly as possible.

Call for Assistance

There are occasional situations when teachers must request assistance in dealing with discipline problems. Some student behaviors by virtue of their intensity, frequency, or bizarre nature demand that the teacher seek the support or assistance of others. "They are intrusive behaviors which uniformly, and almost automatically disrupt the teacher's process; the teacher's response to them must be immediate" (Alley et al., 1990, p. 69). Smith and Misra (1992) suggest that teachers make at least two attempts to manage the behavior themselves before seeking help. In such a case teachers would be able to:
- describe the exact nature of the student's difficulty and the extent to which it deviates from expectations.
- describe antecedent and consequent techniques employed, and
- document the limited effect of these techniques (p. 368).

Examples of situations where teachers might seek assistance include overt, persistent defiance; acts of violence; or anything that threatens the safety of the class.

If teachers are to be effective disciplinarians, they must have the unqualified support of their supervisors and administrators. If a teacher requests assistance, administrative response must be immediate and decisive. If students, especially those inclined to be troublesome, realize that their teacher will receive complete support from the administration, they will be less inclined to disrupt.

It goes without saying that it is very important for teachers not to abuse the process by sending students to the office or calling for assistance for any but the most serious of reasons. Similarly, teachers should not threaten students with being sent to the principal's office whenever there is a problem of any kind in the classroom. In those situations where the problem cannot be handled by the teacher in the classroom, the teacher should, without undo elaboration, call for assistance or send the disrupting student directly to the office. Most discipline situations should, of course, be handled by the teacher in the classroom.

INVOLVE THE PARENTS

It is always a good idea to involve parents in the discipline strategies you employ. Very often parents and teachers working together can produce more effective changes in a student's behavior than either party can when attacking the problem alone. Involving parents also helps avoid the unhappy situation of having a parent call the principal and inquire as to what is going on in the classroom. Frequently, parents hear a distorted explanation of the problem and the teacher's attempts at dealing with the problem from their child. Teachers and parents working together inevitably produces the best solutions.

Another reason to involve the parents is the fact that often the parent is looking for help in dealing with similar displays of behavior at home. Parents often look to the school for assistance in such matters. In attempting to help parents whose children had been identified as discipline or behavioral problems, McCree-Weekly (1995) set up a parent training program to help parents deal with such problems. The parents were at a loss as to how to effectively manage their children's behavior. They were instructed in the use of behavior modification strategies and provided with the opportunity to discuss their experiences and interact with each other.

The most popular strategy with parents was time-out; other options like limit setting, revoking privileges, and record keeping were also popular. However, contingency contracting was not chosen as a preferred activity.

A general observation by the investigator was that prior to parent training students were typically sent to the office for biting and fighting; however, after parent training the most frequent infractions were inattentiveness and failure to remain on task.

Perhaps it can be concluded that schools and teachers can be a valuable asset in helping parents deal with discipline problems in the home. Maybe periodic discussions of the strategies that teachers successfully employ in the classroom will help parents by showing them that they can also successfully employ the same strategies.

REFERENCES

Albert, L.: Discipline: Is it a dirty word? *Learning,* 43–46, 1995.

Alley, R., O'Hair, M., and Wright, R.: Student misbehaviors: Which ones really trouble teachers? *Teacher Education Quarterly, 17*(3), 63–70, 1990

Bender, W. N., and Mathes, M. Y.: Students with ADHD in the inclusive classroom: A hierarchical approach to strategy selection. *Intervention in School and Clinic, 30* (4), 226–234, 1995.

Freiberg, H. J., Stein, T. A., and Parker G.: Discipline referrals in an urban middle school: Implications for discipline and instruction. *Education and Urban Society, 27*(4), 421–440, 1995.

Kann, M. E.: Discipline, character, education. *Teaching Education, 6*(1), 71–75, 1994

Kounin, J.: *Discipline and Group Management in the Classroom.* New York, Holt Rinehart, 1970.

Lawrence, P. A., and Olvey, S. K.: Discipline: A skill not a punishment. *American School Board Journal, 181*(7), 31–32, 1994.

McCain, A. P. and Kelley, M. L.: Improving classroom performance in underachieving preadolescents: The additive effects of response cost to a school-home note system. *Child & Family Behavior Therapy, 16*(2), 27–41, 1994.

McCree-Weekly, E.: Helping parents deal with the discipline of their children through a parent support group. Practicum Report: Nova Southeastern University, ERIC Document ED 387237, 1995.

Reissman, R.: Creative solutions to discipline dilemmas. *Learning, 22*(4), 48–50, 1993.

Rogers, B., 5 tricky personalities and how to handle them. *Instructor.* 16–25, 1995.

Salend, S. J., Tintle, L. and Balber, H.: Effects of a student-managed response-cost system on the behavior of two mainstreamed students. *The Elementary School Journal, 89* (1), 89_97, 1988.

Smith, M. and Misra, A.: A comprehensive management system for students in regular classrooms. *Elementary School Journal, 92*(3), 353–372, 1992.

Chapter 6

DISCIPLINE VIGNETTES

This chapter provides vignettes of actual discipline experiences of real teachers. The teachers are either early in their careers or student teachers who are engaging in their first full-time teaching experience. The vignettes were written by the teachers themselves, and reflect their actual experiences. Each vignette is followed by a reaction to the manner in which the situation was handled and suggestions for more appropriate ways that the teacher could have responded or additional strategies the teachers could have employed.

Female second-year teacher in suburban middle school.

The scenario:

The student was an eighth-grade male who was a difficult student throughout the year for most of his teachers but was usually fairly well behaved in Tech. Ed. Typical disruptive behaviors of the student included refusal to do class work, refusal to bring materials to class, cursing, or using inappropriate language. Typical responses to his deportment were time-outs (requested by either the student or the teacher), lunch detention, after-school detention, or removal from the classroom by an administrator. Academically, he was failing most of his classes, including Tech. Ed.

The student came into class and he asked for a time-out immediately. I told him he could sit in the hall during warm-up (5–10 minutes) but that he would have to come back in for the activity. He agreed, and after the warm-up I asked him to come back in the room. During the directions for the activity, he began commenting inappropriately to other students and to me. I sent him out for a second time-out (5 minutes).

When the rest of the class began the assignment, I went out to talk to the student to find out why he did not want to participate. He said he just didn't feel like being in the class today. I gave him one more chance to come back into the room and participate. He again came in, but would not do the work, so I gave him an after-school detention for not participating. After a few minutes, he went to the paper cutter (available to students doing the class work) and chopped up the detention form. I then called the administrator and had him taken out of the classroom.

The whole episode took about 45 minutes to escalate. The student had a point in saying that if I had just left him in the hallway, he would never have erupted and have to be removed from the room. However, I believed that he should be required to do the class work just like the rest of the students.

The student should not have been allowed to request a "time-out." This situation was apparently more reinforcing to the student than the classroom. The subsequent inappropriate comments should have resulted in a less intrusive strategy such as attempting to generate interest or focusing on something the student values rather than in another time-out. Sitting with the student and asking why he didn't want to participate could well have been reinforcing the inappropriate behavior because of the attention the student was receiving from the teacher.

Female 2nd year teacher in suburban elementary school.

The scenario:

During my first year of teaching, I encountered a student who lacked motivation when completing independent work in Language Arts. This student was an eight-year-old male. The setting was typically at a table of four students during seatwork.

Usually independent work consisted of three activities: one written response, one oral response, and one silent reading activity. This student usually completed only one activity and many times had to be continually redirected or moved to a single desk to complete just that task.

This student slumped in his seat, would whisper to others around him, play with his pencil, ask to use the restroom, and walk around the room. He tended to be on task during group time.

I immediately contacted his parents. After speaking with his parents I created a behavior/academic progress card in which the student had to meet the goal of completing his work. This student wanted to work for a candy treat. If he completed his work he received candy; if not, there was no treat. A parent signature was required each evening. In addition, I spoke with the guidance counselor who suggested that the student come to his office to complete his work during Specials (which were immediately after Language Arts). I did occasionally send him to the guidance counselor's office. The Special Education teacher also came in to complete an evaluation to rule out any type of situation that may have fallen under Special Education laws.

This student used the card all year long, and did progress in completing his work.

Comments:

During independent work the teacher might have chosen to rein-force those students who were working well independently, and attempt to ignore the boy's inappropriate behavior. Any attempt on the part of the boy to try to work independently should result in immediate reinforcement from the teacher. Also, the student may well value the teacher's respect and work to earn it. "Motivation" could be developed by employing a more consistent schedule of reinforce-ment with the boy's target behaviors.

First-year male elementary teacher in an urban elementary school.

The scenario:

I teach at a school where 99 percent of the student popula-tion is minority. The median income of the families in my school is below poverty level and 95 percent of my students come from single-family homes or foster/stepparent care.

I started out the year teaching two sixth-grade Language Arts classes of sixteen students. Two weeks into the school year my principal asked me if I would move to fourth. The female teacher in fourth-grade could not handle the disci-pline problems or the parental attitudes involved with that grade. I volunteered to take the departmentalized fourth-grade Language Arts position and I was in for a surprise. All senior teachers at the school told me that the fourth-grade class has been the worst discipline problem since they began kindergarten. I began teaching them with an open mind.

My most difficult behavioral problem is an African American student who comes from a single-parent family. I will call him X. He is nine years old. I taught his brother for two weeks in sixth grade. His brother is eleven. I will call him Y. His brother and I became friends. He has helped me handle the problems with X.

It began on a normal day in early October. X's class came in and began their warm-up. He had yet to possess a warm-up journal and that day I gave him a piece of paper to begin. He had several pens and pencils that he brought to my class. Instead of doing warm-up, he sat and played with a pen and a pencil. I took the pen away from him. I told him to start doing his warm up. He refused and began playing with the rest of his pens and pencils. As I was going over the warm-up, I walked over to him. He continued to play with his pens and pencils. I tried to take all but one pencil away from him. He would not give them to me so I grabbed them from his hand. He squeezed harder and I yanked them out of his hand. He sat back in his chair and put his feet on his desk. I asked him to sit properly and he complied hesitantly. I sat his pens and pencils on the chalkboard ledge. As we were finishing our warm-up and beginning whole group, he walked up and grabbed his pens and pencils as I was helping another student. I marched over to his desk and took them out of his hand and placed them in my desk drawer. He sat down screaming "I don't care. I will have my mother come up here and take them from you." I stated "Bring your mother up! I will welcome a conference with her." At that moment he sat back down and began to do some work. He really never started his work, but he sat there quietly enough so I could teach the class. He still was a distraction to me and the rest of my students.

One half hour before the class was leaving my room (we have two-hour blocks) he began to play with the one pencil he had left. He would bang the desk with the pencil as he rocked back on his chair. I asked him to stop and he didn't. He is very stubborn and would not reason. I told him he would get his pens and pencils back at the end of the day. I grabbed the only pencil he had out of his hand as he continued to defy me. He kicked his desk three feet across the room. I told him to leave my classroom, take his books, and go next door to the new sixth-grade teacher's room. I asked him three times, screaming the last time. He would not listen. I threatened to call the office. At this time he said his normal phrase "I am not doing anything wrong! You better give me my pencils back now!" I told him that I was the teacher. What I do or say is final and have a seat. I began to write an Office Referral. He picked up his chair and threw it down, almost striking another student. I grabbed his arm to take him out of the classroom. He picked up his books with his other arm and threw them across the room, hitting the door. He ran to the corner of the room, jumped up, and sat on the counter in front of the window and began to cry. Only several minutes were left in class. I left him there until class was over and I could complete the Office Referral. He seemed stable there and I did not want to cause any more problems. I lined up the class and took them to the math teacher across the hall. X remained on the window ledge.

After calling his mother, my principal suspended him for two days. Later that day I saw his older brother and told him about the incident and asked him to tell his mom. He did! I have had several meetings with his mother since then to deal with the child's behavior. He has been suspended twice because of his behavior. His mother is called in at least twice a month to handle the child. She is not a disciplinarian, but rather a talker and bargainer with her children. Lately he is doing better. He still can come into the classroom with an attitude, but not like that day.

Comments:

Certainly the strategy of ignoring inappropriate behavior and reinforcing incompatible behavior should be diligently attempted. Also, students near him engaging in appropriate behavior should be reinforced so that he is vicariously reinforced for appropriate behavior.

The teacher should not have engaged the child in debate. Once a teacher does this, she has lost. In situations like this there is nothing to debate. Simply impose the appropriate disciplinary action and move on.

Female student teacher in a suburban high school.

The scenario:

The most unusual discipline problem that I have experienced occurred within the first month of my student teaching experience. The student involved was a ninth grade female. She talked a lot during class and had a slight "attitude" at the beginning of the year. This particular day my cooperating teacher had left the room to run down to the office. The students' assignment was a difficult worksheet, and many students had questions. This particular student called out "Hey you!" I looked at her and she eventually raised her hand. I then moved across the room to help a student who had her hand raised the entire time. The problem student began complaining, and I told her I'd be over as soon as I was finished. When I finally went over to help her she said she was waiting for my cooperating teacher. I walked away frustrated and upset. Then I thought about it and talked about the situation with my mentor teacher. We decided that I should issue the student a detention for attitude and disruptive behavior. Before class began the next day, I asked her to come outside the room with me. Then I handed her the form and told her it was for her behavior yesterday and asked her to sign it. She began to argue with me and I said we can discuss this tomorrow when you're here after school. She then signs the form. The following afternoon when she came in for detention she said "Hi" to the coop teacher and glared at me. The following day she told me that she really enjoyed the unit we were studying. She seems to have become my friend and definitely respects me.

Comments:

The detention that was ultimately given to the student was not immediate and the impact of immediate reinforcement was lost. At first, the student teacher should have ignored the misbehaving student and ultimately used the opportunity to practice the "I mean business look." Another possibility would be to try to generate interest in the student. The fact that the student came around and worked well with the student teacher suggests that the student teacher may well have been able to be an influencing variable in the student's life.

Female student teacher in a suburban middle school.

The scenario:

Phillip was a very difficult student. He was already repeating eighth grade and almost never came to school. He lived with his grandmother who worked early in the morning, so when he got up for school there was no one at home to make him go—and often he would not. I think Phillip knew that regardless he would go on to the ninth grade because the state law says you can't be held back two times.

I know through team teacher meetings that Phillip's attendance was a real problem. When I began teaching, I decided to observe how many days in a row he would come to school in the next week. I told myself I would praise him if he came consecutively for three days. Surprisingly, he showed up for school all week! On Friday, I called him over to me after class. I told him how glad I was to see him in class and I hoped it would continue. I must say that it did improve. However, Phillip's behavior was a problem, too. He gave me the most confrontational situation of my student teaching experience.

In class one day, I saw Phillip writing on another child. I told him to stop doing it, or he would be "out of my classroom." He continued, of course, because he thought I would

not follow through with my promise. (I had never sent someone to the principal before.) At this point, I asked "Phil, do
you want to sit in the corner desk by yourself? The class is set
up in groups of 4, but there is a table at the back corner
where no one sits.

He shouted, "NO!" The class got quiet and he started
smirking. I said "Phil, I think you should pick up your books
and move to the empty desk. You don't seem capable of
working with your group today." Again, he said, "NO!"

I responded by saying, "You will have to go to the office
then." He defiantly said "NO!" once more. Remaining calm,
I walked over to the intercom and called down to the office.
I asked for someone to "remove a young man from my classroom."

He was quiet for me from that day on and he continued to
show up for school. He even apologized to me after school
one day when he was waiting for his bus!

Comments:

*The first reprimand was very appropriate; clearly the misbehav-
ing student had to be stopped from writing on another student.
However, the threat of removal turned out to be hollow. The student
was not removed but was isolated instead. This scenario provides a
good example of how calling for assistance, even though it was rather
late, was an effective strategy.*

Female first-year teacher in a suburban elementary school.

The scenario:

I have a group of six special education students in my
class. One of the girls, in addition to having learning problems, is diagnosed as violently aggressive. Physically she is
extremely mature for her age. She is nine years old, in the
third grade as big as I am.

While walking in gym one day she called the back half of the line "stupid morons" which of course upset my class. So I had a talk with her about respect and treating others the way you want to be treated. After school that day my class was still wound up over it and as far as I can tell they were just looking at her (she really does hate to be looked at) and she pinned a student up against a wall. I defused that by "you sit here, you stay away," etc.

The next day she was trying to play soccer with my class. She got mad because they wouldn't let her have the ball so she hit one of the boys. He came up and told me (not very upset; he's an instigator). I told him to bring her up and I'd get both stories. He never came back, and I went after them both. By this time the boy was playing again and she was chasing another child saying "you wanta be next? I'll hit you too!" I called all three people over and asked, "What's going on?" All three started at once, so I said, "One at a time."

Every time one of the boys started she'd yell and interrupt. So I pulled each aside while the other two were sitting in the grass. Next thing I know she's up walking across the soccer field! "Karla, I'm not finished with you, you need to come back." "My name isn't Karla," she said. "I don't care what your name is I told her (it is Karla) get back here!" So I had to follow her as she's leaving the playground. Finally, I stopped saying anything and just walked a little behind her. I did say before I stopped talking I thought she needed to pay the support room a visit.

When I got her turned in the right direction I walked ahead of her without a word and she did follow. She continued up and stood by the fence for the rest of recess. I didn't make her go to the support room because the power struggle (go or not go) would have started again. I found with her it is best to let her think she's getting her way although she isn't. Ignoring the behavior (walking away) brought her around to do as I asked (go back where you belong). There's a definite personality clash happening with her and two or three of my regular education students.

Comments:

It was not a good idea to ask the boy to bring the misbehaving girl to the teacher. The teacher should have gone to get the girl. When the girl walked away from her, the teacher's reprimand was quite appropriate.

The teacher saying to the girl, "I think you need to go to the support room" and then not making her actually go was inappropriate.

Always avoid power struggles; never debate with a misbehaving student. It would also be valuable to attempt to find out what this student values and attempt to use that in discipline strategies. Removal to a time-out situation or some form of response-cost would also have been appropriate in this situation.

Female first-year teacher in a suburban elementary school.

The scenario:

This problem occurred with a 10-year-old boy in my fifth-grade class. The boy is a very intelligent, outgoing, and charismatic character; his main goal in life is to star in a movie, and I am certain that he will one day achieve this! He has been the class clown ever since kindergarten and has informed me that a few years ago he was "really bad" and his current behavior is, by comparison, "pretty good."

I had ongoing problems with his behavior in the first month of school because of his constant quest to entertain the class. The last straw came when he completely disrupted our Language Arts group one day by writing the word "FART" in huge letters on the back of his notebook and holding it up for his friends to see. I told him to go sit in time-out at the other end of the room, and I had him turn a card. (I have a card system; they turn cards when they break a rule.) The immediate result was that he sulked in the time-out area for a while, then he returned to the group and was no longer disruptive.

I knew that I had to do something to stop the overall disruptive pattern, or it would just continue to get worse. The parents told me that they would back me up on anything I tried; they were well aware of their son's record. I spoke to his teacher from the previous year, who told me that he had more success when this boy was seated away from the other students.

I was tired of constantly issuing negative consequences to this boy, and I knew he was tired of it as well. I made a small, inconspicuous behavior card to put on his desk. For each class period in which he was on-task, he would receive a sticker. I talked about it with him and he set his own goal, which was to receive four stickers per day, or twenty per week. He chose his own reward, which was to perform a monologue from a play in front of the class.

The behavior card system worked fairly well, but there were times when he was still totally off task and did not seem to care whether he received a sticker. One day after school I separated his desk from the others, and that seemed to help because he no longer had an audience.

Comments:

The time-out strategy employed by the teacher was a good choice in this situation. It was also an excellent idea to talk to the parents and the child's previous teachers. The use of stickers as a form of reinforcement for appropriate behavior is a good and workable strategy. However, it should be coupled with an intrusive strategy such as time-out until the appropriate behavior becomes firmly established. The "audience" of the class was obviously providing powerful reinforcement to him when he acted out.

Female student teacher in a suburban elementary school.

The scenario:

I was substituting for my mentor today. The first class we have is Social Studies. I was doing one of my own lesson plans. Many students asked where Mrs. H was. I announced to the whole class that she would not be here today but might visit at the end of the day.

There were two boys that I had to remind more than enough times during the lesson to either be quiet or stop doing something that they should not have been doing. The students who can not see the board are allowed to come up to the front tables. These two boys were ones that usually move. This is nothing out of the ordinary. Sometimes, they may sit next to each other depending on who else is at the table and where the others may choose to sit. Today, they sat next to each other.

The one boy has ADHD. His mother decided to try him without his medicine this year. When my mentor called parents before school started, his mother described him as someone who calls out and is impulsive. We had an IEP for him. He is not one who causes a lot of trouble in our classroom and is a good student, but he does call out a lot.

The other boy is very unorganized and has been having difficulty staying on task. He struggles with following directions and keeping up with the rest of the class. After he put a paper I gave him in his binder, he started going through the rest of his binder. I reminded him to stay with us, and I flipped his binder to the page we were on.

Throughout the lesson, the first boy would call out answers. Many times I would remind him to raise his hand or I would praise someone else for raising his or her hand. However, there were times I would accept his answer.

The two boys did not interact throughout the lesson until the end. I had given them plenty of individual warnings. As soon as I saw a problem, I corrected them and said that next time they would have to flip their cards. The second boy immediately tried to give me excuses.

After Social Studies, the class went to their specials, and two students had to flip their cards. It was the two boys I had repeatedly warned.

I should have had them flip their cards, but I did not want to bring attention to them or make it into something bigger than it was. I always hesitate, and by the time I decide to discipline, it is too late. I could have had them move back to their original seats and away from each other.

Comments:

It most certainly would have been a good idea to have them move back to their original seats and be separated from one another. It also appears that the teacher provided too many "reminders." These often serve as positive reinforcement of the inappropriate behavior. The teacher must work to be consistent and not accept call-outs when the rule is that hands must be raised. With a "card system" as described above, the teacher should not warn or threaten. It is better to just go and flip the misbehaving student's card.

Female student teacher in a suburban elementary school.

The scenario:

On October 27, 1998, at 11:30 am Brutus, an eight-year-old boy, was misbehaving. The other third graders had come into the room from the computer lab. They were working on independent work that I had assigned to them. Brutus was the only student who was not following directions. I went over to him and asked him to take out his graphic organizer (that was due 2 1/2 weeks earlier) and for him to write his rough draft paragraph. Brutus made no response to me. He turned his head when I tried to talk to him. He glared at me for a couple of minutes and showed disrespect towards me.

I then told Brutus that he could do his work during afternoon break, but he still did not comply. After about ten minutes, I called the students to sit over at the rocking chair. Brutus would not move out of his chair. I gave him warnings that consisted of missing recess the entire week, calling home and finally going down to the office. I heard him say under his breath, "I don't care." At that point I told him that another student's instructional aide could take him down to the office if he did not join the group. After no response, I wrote up a referral on him because of his attitude. After no response, he still would not go to the office and he was now in more trouble. The instructional aide who is always in our classroom went to ask the vice principal to come to get him.

It was then time for lunch. I called groups to line up and Brutus got in line. I told him that he was not going to lunch with us. I walked the students down to lunch while our vice principal came to get Brutus.

Comments:

In this scenario too many warnings and threats were issued. This might have been a situation where a continued effort to generate interest would have improved the situation. Most certainly an unsuccessful stern reprimand should be followed by time-out or some type of response-cost.

Female student teacher in a suburban elementary school.

The scenario:

This semester I am student teaching in a second-grade classroom. I have a very diverse class in that most are on grade level and about nine are identified as special education students. Just recently one of my special education students has been very disruptive. I have had to send six notes home in the past eleven school days because she has landed on that spot in our behavior management system. First, you move your dart to a warning. Next, you lose recess. Then you have a letter sent home. Finally, if it moves again in the same day, you are referred to the principal's office.

I sent this student to the principal's office yesterday with a referral. I also sent a note home explaining what had happened. Today, her behavior was just about the same. Although she was not out of her seat as much, she did many things that caused her dart to be moved. Today, she sang an inappropriate song for school, and picked up another student while walking down the hall. She was very talkative and called out too many times. Each time, I warned her that those actions were not appropriate for school and her dart would be moved. She also wrote "I love you" on another student's work. At that I said, "Maybe you need to make another trip to the principal's office." She shook her head no and put out her bottom lip. Then I said, "Better yet, maybe I should just make a phone call to your father at work right now. That way, you can explain to him what you have done today." This time she said, "NO! NO! I don't want you to call him." I said, "The next time I even have to think about correcting you, I am calling your father."

Amazingly, she was not disruptive for the rest of the day (which was only the last period). She participated in our Native American lesson, she was quiet, and she left the other students alone. I sent a note home with her, explaining what had happened today. Attached to the note I put a copy of the behavior card I made up for this student. After yesterday, I decided she needed something extra to make her experience at school more positive. This behavior card will give her something tangible to strive for, rather than trying not to lose something such as recess. I asked her father for any suggestions or comments he may have about the behavior card. I hope this improves her behavior . . . soon!

Comments:

Obviously this misbehaving girl "values" not having her father called. The teacher is quite correct in recognizing the need to create a system of positive reinforcement to use with the girl. The existing system is appropriate in that it progresses from less intrusive to more intrusive, but it must be accompanied by a system of reinforcing behaviors that are incompatible with the misbehaviors.

Female student teacher in suburban elementary school.

The scenario:

For my on-grade-level math group, six students from other second-grade classrooms come over to ours. These students are usually never a problem. If I have to correct them, it never has gone past a warning. However, today was a little different. One student in particular was extremely distracted and was acting out. After several of my "glances" and warnings, I told Rick that if he acted out again, he would owe me recess. I had given him enough warnings. That seemed to calm him down . . . for about one minute.

After doing a few more math problems with the students, I looked over and noticed Rick on the ground with his shirt over his knees. I said "Rick, you have until I count to five to sit up and pay attention." As I started counting, he made a big commotion like he was stuck. I replied, "You will owe me recess tomorrow too." He still took his time getting out of his shirt. So I told him he would owe me recess.

I also told him to keep it up and he would continue to owe me recess for the whole week. He calmed down a little, but not enough. At this point I was getting annoyed. Recess did not seem enough. So after he began singing aloud I made him go back to his seat. I said, "You will not continue to disrupt this class; you may leave the group and watch from your desk." He walked back to his desk with his head down. After group was over, I called him over to me and asked him what was wrong. I wanted to know why he felt the need to distract the whole math group. He said he did not know. So I told him that was unacceptable and the next time something like this happened, he would take a trip to the principal's office.

When he came in during his class recess, I could tell he had been crying. He really did not want to give up recess. As much as I hate to see a child cry, I think he needs to learn to pay the price for his actions. So, I will see him tomorrow for recess as well.

Comments:

It was quite appropriate to begin with "the glance" and then to actually move to the problem. The teacher should continue to try to ascertain elements of the child's environment that he truly values, so that they can be used constructively to improve any discipline problems. The "response-cost" feature of this scenario was excellent. The teacher might need to be reminded, however, that it is not appropriate to withdraw a penalty once it has been given. When you tell a student that he will miss recess, you must follow through.

Female student teacher in a suburban elementary school.

The scenario:

It began when I was walking the class to P.E. class. I was at the end of the line. Mrs. B was at the front. Andy was at the end, right behind me. Out of the corner of my eye I saw him side kick another student. I turned quickly and told him what I saw. He said that the boy hurt him first. I told him that his card would be moved. He did not like the sound of this. He replied: "I might as well have my older brother teach me. This school is so stupid. Why am I here?" After hearing such comments, I pulled him away from the class and told him that we would have a nice talk after P.E. He stomped away.

I told Mrs. B of the incident. She agreed that I should have a talk with him. After forty minutes, I returned to pick up the class from the gymnasium without Mrs. B. The students were quietly waiting. A substitute stood in front of them and told me of another incident Andy caused in class. Apparently he kicked another student and punched the P.E. teacher in the stomach. The rest of the students wanted to tell me everything. I had to calm them before leaving the room. We walked to the end of the hallway. I turned around and saw him catching up to the class. It looked normal.

Suddenly he began throwing himself, arm first, into the walls of the hallway. Side-to-side this boy was literally bouncing off the walls. I had to stop him. I told him to stop and stand in line, but that had no effect. As classes were traveling through the hallways a first-grade teacher looked on. She asked another teacher if she would take my class to her classroom. I was now alone with Andy in the hallway. He continued to run and bounce off each wall. I finally got hold of him and tightened my arms. I did not want to hurt him. He tried very hard to get away. I did not want to fight it any longer. I let go thinking it would be OK. He went back to his bouncing. I was scared. There was nothing I could do to make him stop. I told him that we would go to the office and talk with the principal. I told him that he can tell her what is bothering him. He did not say a word. He just kept hitting the walls. I was now afraid that he would break something, like his arm.

The school secretary walked down the hallway. I had him in a hold and asked her if the principal was available. She said "No, she is at a meeting right now, but the vice principal is in her office." Knowing that I wanted to get him there, I said that we were on our way. She nodded and left. I continued to hold him as he struggled to break free. He kicked, stomped, and elbowed me many times. He told me that he would do karate on me and it would hurt. I told him that I did not want to hurt him. I asked him why he wanted to hurt me? I got no response. After some time, he stopped his struggle. I pushed him against the wall and had him sit down. I said "Let's calm down and talk about what is wrong. You can calm down and relax." He sat down and I loosened my grip. He seemed OK so I pulled away. I sat down across from him. He had his arms crossed and just stared at the floor. Then, before I knew it he jumped up and began running. I told him to get back and stop. He did not listen. I began running. Without knowing it, I looked up and he was heading out the front door. I was too scared for words. I thought to myself "He is leaving the building, what do I do?" We got outside and he stopped. He knew he was not supposed to be there. I began screaming at the top of my lungs. He knew I was not just upset but scared. I know I was hot, red, and teary-eyed. He could see it. He slowly began walking back towards me, still grunting with his arms crossed. I quickly grabbed him and carried him into the building.

As we walked toward the office, the teachers who walked by could see the anger in him and the fear in me. I took a break and regained my grip on him. He began kicking me again. Then, Mrs. W came down the hallway. She saw my face and quickly grabbed his feet. We carried him the rest of the way to the office. As we were walking, he punched her in the arm. She said "That didn't hurt." When we got to the office the principal and vice principal were standing there with their arms out. I handed him over and he fell to the ground. He began screaming: "I want to go home." The principal said she would take it from there. I left the room relieved and shook up.

Teachers began coming over to me and helping me calm down. They told me stories to make me laugh and gave me advice. They were understanding and approving of what I had done. I was still scared. I went into the bathroom and let everything out that had built up in me. I did not want to return to the classroom teary-eyed or red.

I had male teachers tell me what they would have done, but the female teachers gave me confidence and said that what I did was right. They said I handled it just fine. I know I will never forget this experience. I will also never name my child after him.

Comments:

This was obviously an extremely frightening situation for any teacher, much less a student teacher. It is perfectly understandable that student teachers, indeed most teachers, want to handle disruptive situations themselves, but there are times when discretion is the better part of valor. This was a situation where she should have called for assistance early on in the episode. The potential for physical harm to the student teacher as well as the potential for the harm that could have befallen the student, especially when he actually left the building, clearly indicates that she should have called for assistance.

Chapter 7

THEORETICAL FOUNDATION OF STUDENT DISCIPLINE

Behavior is what students do; anything and everything they do in and out of the classroom is a form of human behavior. Examples of student behavior are:
- Writing answers to mathematics problems
- Hand-raising during an oral activity
- Open discussion of a selected topic
- Seat leaving
- Arguing
- Fighting

If student discipline problems are defined as actions by students that disrupt the learning effectiveness or safety of the classroom, it can easily be recognized that student discipline problems are a form of human behavior. Such behaviors are called operants or operant behavior and unlike respondent behavior are not caused by a stimulus. Rather they are occasioned by a special type of stimulus which is known as a *discriminative stimulus*. Operant behaviors are emitted in the presence of a discriminative stimulus because of the students' history of consequences associated with that behavior. For example when Ms. Smith (discriminative stimulus) says to a group of students, "Settle down and take out your workbooks", the students quiet down and take out their books (operant behavior). This behavior is supported by their history of dealing with Ms. Smith. On the other hand, if Ms. Jones (discriminative stimulus) says the same thing, the same group of students might continue to talk and socialize (operant behavior). Their behavior is sustained by their history of dealing with Ms. Jones. It is important to understand that it is the consequences of operant behavior that establish and maintain the behavior. It is typically unproductive to blame student misbehavior on some hypothetical construct. For example, it would not be productive for Ms. Jones to blame the students' failure to respond to her directive as a lack of motivation or an absence of readiness skills.

In terms of discipline problems, it is certainly the case that misbehavior, acting out, and fighting are all forms of operant behavior and as such are established and sustained by reinforcers that are provided by the environment. In most cases the child's environment is providing reinforcers naturally and in many cases unintentionally. Nicole's laughing at Erica when she makes a funny noise is a positive reinforcer in Erica's environment and serves to strengthen her inappropriate behavior. Similarly the teacher's scolding Teddy for not paying attention is, although unintentionally, reinforcing that behavior by providing attention to the inappropriate behavior. The challenge for the teacher is to conceptualize and implement a system of classroom management that includes providing positive reinforcement for appropriate behavior (i.e., behavior incompatible with the misbehavior) and weakening consequences for misbehavior. Weakening consequences can take the form of extinction, where positive reinforcement for inappropriate behavior is withheld, or punishment where an aversive consequence is provided contingent on the misbehavior, or earned reinforcement is removed contingent on the misbehavior. As was discussed in Chapter 5, the actions by the teacher can range from nonintrusive to very intrusive. Table 7.1 provides a review of possible actions.

Table 7.1
DECREASING INAPPROPRIATE BEHAVIOR

Nonintrusive		More Intrustive
• Add aversive consequence	• Deliver a stern glance • Move to students location	• Assign detention • Give time-out
• Remove earned positive reinforcers	• Delete earned points • Ask to perform an errand such as handing out workbooks	• Call for assistance • Refuse permission to attend an assembly • Deny recess

Once the concept of student discipline problems as forms of operant behavior is understood and embraced, it is relatively easy to comprehend that these operant behaviors will respond to a system of operant conditioning or consequence management. Often referred to as behavior modification or behavior management, the objective is to manage the consequences of a student's behavior to bring about a more appropriate behavioral repertoire. Once new, appropriate behaviors become established, it is expected that the teacher will "stretch the schedule" of reinforcement to decrease the student's dependency on extrinsic reinforcers. More will be said about this later.

In dealing with behaviors which are examples of discipline problems, the teacher's goal is typically to increase the frequency or intensity of behaviors that are incompatible with the misbehavior and to decrease the frequency or intensity of the inappropriate behavior. The manner in which these goals are accomplished is depicted in Table 7.2. Before addressing the actual application of consequences, it is imperative to emphasize that the consequences must be applied immediately. In other words, as soon as a teacher observes an inappropriate behavior, she must provide the consequence at once. Similarly, when she observes a behavior that is incompatible with the misbehavior, she must provide the strengthening consequence at that moment.

Table 7.2
EFFECT OF CONSEQUENCES ON BEHAVIOR

Increase Behavior Reinforcement	
Positive Reinforcement	*Negative Reinforcement*
Provide a pleasing or preferred consequence to the student	Remove an aversive or undesirable consequence from the student

Decrease Behavior		
Punishment		*Extinction*
Punishment by Addition	*Punishment by Subtraction*	
Provide an aversive consequences to the student	Response-cost strategy	Remove or prevent positive reinforcement

In addressing the goal of decreasing inappropriate behavior, teachers can employ punishment or extinction. There are two ways to employ the principle of punishment. The first type of punishment is the application of an aversive consequence. For example, if a teacher observes George punch Emilio, she could immediately inform George that he had been given a detention. The second type of punishment is where earned reinforcement is removed contingent upon a misbehavior. For example, the teacher, on seeing George hit Emilio, could immediately remove points or tokens George had earned for appropriate behavior. This is commonly known as response-cost.

The other way to decrease behavior is by manipulating the environment so as to allow extinction to occur. This means that positive reinforcement is removed or not provided. A teacher who consistently ignores Jennifer's persistently talking out without being recognized, is allowing extinction to occur. In other words, the inappropriate behavior of talking out is consistently ignored and will ultimately extinguish or disappear.

Consistent with the strategies of decreasing inappropriate behavior, are the strategies of increasing behaviors that are incompatible with the inappropriate behavior. The most common method of accomplishing this is positive reinforcement. An immediate application of a positive consequence contingent upon appropriate behavior is positive reinforcement. If Jennifer does raise her hand before talking out, the teacher should immediately call on her or provide her with a token or a point on her score sheet. This, when done consistently, will result in an increase in her hand-raising behavior.

Another method of increasing behavior is through the process of negative reinforcement. It is important to understand that this is not the same thing as punishment. As a matter of fact, one way to think of negative reinforcement is as the removal of punishment. Technically, negative reinforcement is the removal or avoidance of an aversive consequence. For example, if Zack is able to avoid the aversive consequence of homework over the weekend by finishing his essay in class, his on-task behavior will increase. It will increase as a result of negative reinforcement.

Not only is it important to understand the effect of consequences on behavior, it is also crucial to understand how those consequences are applied. The manner in which consequences are applied is most often referred to as *schedules of reinforcement.*

The goal of manipulating the consequences of behavior is to change that behavior. Generally speaking, the target objective is usually to establish, maintain, increase, decrease, or eliminate a behavior. A different schedule of reinforcement is called for depending on the target.

Before delving very deeply into the topic of schedules of reinforcement, it is appropriate to consider how behavior is measured. For the most part, behavior is measured by counting its frequency or duration. In other words, how many times does Hector speak out without being called upon (frequency) or how long does Hector remain off task when he is assigned seatwork (duration)? Once the issue of how behavior will be measured is addressed, it is appropriate to examine the schedules of delivering reinforcement.

SCHEDULE OF REINFORCEMENT

The term schedule of reinforcement is used to describe the delivery of reinforcement contingent upon the occurrence of a specified number of behaviors or upon the first occurrence of a behavior after the passage of a specified amount of time.

Fixed Ratio Schedule

The term *fixed ratio* indicates that the reinforcement will be delivered on a ratio basis. In other words, a predetermined number of occurrences of the behavior must occur before reinforcement is delivered. The word fixed indicates that the number of occurrences is consistent. An example would be a fixed ratio of three (FR3). This means that reinforcement is contingent on every three occurrences of the behavior. When attempting to establish a new behavior, it is best to employ a continuous schedule (FR1). In other words every occurrence of the behavior is reinforced. For example if a teacher is attempting to establish hand-raising behavior in

Lizzy, she would reinforce her every time she raised her hand. As the behavior became established, the teacher would "stretch the schedule" to FR3 or FR5. Stretching the schedule is an important strategy because it prevents satiation (essentially tiring of the reinforcer) and minimizes the possibility of extinction occurring if reinforcement is inadvertently interrupted. After a behavior is established and maintained, it is time to move to a more intermittent schedule such as a variable ratio schedule.

Variable Ratio Schedule

A *variable ratio schedule* is similar to the fixed ratio schedule in that it is based on the frequency of the target behavior. The difference is the reinforcement is provided contingent upon varying numbers of occurrences of the behavior. A variable ratio of four (VR4) would mean that reinforcement would be delivered inconsistently but the average would be every four occurrences of the behavior. As Lizzy's hand-raising behavior becomes more firmly established she would be "stretched"; for example, from VR4 to VR6. A behavior reinforced on a VR6 schedule would be extremely resistant to extinction.

A word should be said about the types of reinforcers a teacher chooses to provide. Rather than worry about which primary reinforcers are most effective with each student, it is usually more practical to implement a "token economy" in the classroom where tokens or points are awarded by the teacher. These are easy to award and can be redeemed by the students at a later time. Token economics also prevent students from becoming satiated on a particular reinforcer because students have a menu of items for which they can redeem their earned tokens or points.

Some behaviors lend themselves more to a temporal measurement rather than a frequency measurement. In such cases an interval schedule of reinforcement is used.

Fixed Interval Schedule

A *fixed interval schedule* means that a prescribed amount of time (e.g., three minutes) must elapse and then the next occurrence of the behavior is reinforced. Such a schedule would be depicted as FI3. For example, if a teacher is interested in increasing the amount of time Jessica stays on task, she might put Jessica on a VI2 schedule of reinforcement. This would mean that if after two minutes Jessica was on task, she would be reinforced. This schedule should also be stretched to, for example, FI4 or FI6. Ultimately it would be appropriate to move to a variable schedule.

Variable Interval Schedule

A *variable interval schedule* of reinforcement simply means that the amount of time that must elapse prior to reinforcement varies around some predetermined average. For example, if Alicia were placed on a VI4 schedule of reinforcement, it would mean that she might be reinforced after three minutes, then after six minutes, then after seven minutes, and then after two minutes. The objective is to average about four minutes of time before the target behavior is reinforced. A variable interval schedule of reinforcement makes it exceedingly difficult for the student to anticipate the reinforcement, and consequently, is extremely resistant to extinction.

There are more complicated schedules of reinforcement which combine various forms of ratio and interval schedules. Nevertheless, the four schedules described above provide an overview of the basic schedules of reinforcement.

As a rule of thumb it can be claimed that more consistent schedules of reinforcement are used in establishing a behavior, while more intermittent schedules are employed in maintaining a behavior.

STRETCHING THE SCHEDULE OF REINFORCEMENT

Once a student's inappropriate behavior decreases or an incompatible behavior increases to the target level, it is very important to change the schedule of reinforcement so as to decrease the student's dependency on extrinsic reinforcers. This change in the schedule of reinforcement is known as stretching the schedule and will also serve to prevent extinction from occurring should some circumstance prevent the scheduled delivery of reinforcement.

For example, if Jamal's number of talk outs had been decreased by reinforcing his hand raising every time he raised his hand, it would be necessary to change from an FR1 schedule to FR3 and then to FR5 for example. In other words, the teacher would progressively move to an inconsistent schedule that averaged a reinforcer for every four times Jamal raised his hand.

The idea is to progressively stretch the use of extrinsic reinforcers with the goal of essentially eliminating them. The idea is to build and increase the child's reservoir of intrinsic reinforcers and decrease his reliance on extrinsic reinforcers. The intent is to approximate the schedule of reinforcement and the type of reinforcement provided routinely by the natural environment.

Anyone who responsibly manipulates the consequences of student behavior for the purpose of changing that student's behavior should embrace the goal of the student developing self-control of the target behavior. This, of course, is the ultimate goal of behavior modification.

REINFORCERS

Reinforcers can be either positive or negative. Positive reinforcers are provided in positive reinforcement and removed during extinction. Negative reinforcers are added during punishment and removed or avoided during negative reinforcement. There are many consequences that can serve as positive reinforcers and many that can function as negative reinforcers. However, care must be judiciously exercised to avoid the assumption that a consequence will necessarily function as a positive reinforcer for *all* children. For example, although many children enjoy dried fruit or free time in the art center, Shaniqua might prefer pretzel nuggets or free time to read. If teachers want to change student behavior by providing immediate reinforcers, it is crucial that they determine what consequences are indeed reinforcing for each child. The task of whether a consequence is reinforcing or not is whether or not it results in a change in behavior for the particular child.

Positive reinforcers can be subdivided into extrinsic (seen as outside the child and provided by someone else) and intrinsic (that sense of satisfaction a child feels for a job well done) reinforcers. The teacher's task is to help the child develop his own intrinsic reinforcers. However, in order to do so, it is often necessary to legitimately use extrinsic reinforcers to create a series of appropriate behaviors. Identifying individual, appropriate extrinsic reinforcers highlights the important differences between primary and secondary reinforcers (Table 3).

Table 7.3
REINFORCERS

Reinforcers		
Positive Reinforcers		*Negative Reinforcers*
Extrinsic	Intrinsic	
primary secondary		

Primary reinforcers, in and of themselves, are valued and desired by children. The easiest way to understand primary reinforcers is to think of the value of food to a hungry person. Secondary reinforcers have no inherent value; the actual value of green paper rectangles is obviously very limited. However, people learn to value money, and it quickly takes on a very high value.

The importance of the necessity of learning to value secondary reinforcers cannot be stressed too strongly. If something does not have value to a student, it will not serve as a reinforcer for that student. Tokens awarded to Cathy for on-task behavior may have no value to her until she learns that they can be redeemed for primary reinforcers. Similarly, praise and compliments from the teacher will only have legitimate value to Cathy as she learns to value that particular teacher's opinions.

Regrettably some teachers who are willing to try behavior management begin by employing only secondary reinforcers. If these are not valued by the student, it is easy to see that failure is inevitable.

Everyone has heard the expression "Success breeds success." This old saying is actually a good descriptor of how intrinsic reinforcers are developed; they are not innate. As primary and later secondary reinforcers are employed to change behavior, the delivery of these reinforcers should be accompanied by promise. This will create and increase the value of such praise. It must be emphasized that reinforcers should be delivered only for legitimate success experiences. They should not be delivered "noncontingently" or just to make the child feel good.

The more a child genuinely feels good and truly values the legitimate success experiences she has, the more she will develop intrinsic reinforcers that will allow her to manage her own behavior. This, of course, is the ultimate goal of a good program of behavior management.

REFERENCES

Axelrod, S.: *Behavior Modification* (2nd ed.). New York, McGraw-Hill, 1983

Bellack, A. S., Hersen, M., and Kazdin, A. E.: *International Handbook of Behavior Modification and Therapy.* New York, Plenum Press, 1982.

The Council for Exceptional Children: Managing inappropriate behavior in the classroom. *Eric Digest #E408.* 2–3, 1990.

Kazdin, A. E.: *Behavior Modification.* Chicago, Dorsey Press, 1989.

Matson, J. L., and McCartney, J. R.: *Handbook of Behavior Modification with the Mentally Retarded.* New York, Plenum Press, 1981.

Presbie, R. J., and Brown, P. L.: *Behavior Modification.* Washington, D.C., National Education Association, 1985.

Thompson, T. I. and Grabowski, J.: *Behavior Modification of the Mentally Retarded.* New York, Oxford University Press, 1977.

INDEX